THE EMPIRICISTS:
A GUIDE FOR THE PERPLEXED

Continuum *Guides for the Perplexed*

Continuum's Guides for the Perplexed are clear, concise and accessible introductions to thinkers, writers and subjects that students and readers can find especially challenging. Concentrating specifically on what it is that makes the subject difficult to grasp, these books explain and explore key themes and ideas, guiding the reader towards a thorough understanding of demanding material.

Guides for the Perplexed **available from Continuum:**
Adorno: A Guide for the Perplexed, Alex Thomson
Arendt: A Guide for the Perplexed, Karin Fry
Aristotle: A Guide for the Perplexed, John Vella
Bentham: A Guide for the Perplexed, Philip Schofield
Berkley: A Guide for the Perplexed, Talia Bettcher
Deleuze: A Guide for the Perplexed, Claire Colebrook
Derrida: A Guide for the Perplexed, Julian Wolfreys
Descartes: A Guide for the Perplexed, Justin Skirry
Existentialism: A Guide for the Perplexed, Stephen Earnshaw
Freud: A Guide for the Perplexed, Celine Surprenant
Gadamer: A Guide for the Perplexed, Chris Lawn
Habermas: A Guide for the Perplexed, Eduardo Mendieta
Hegel: A Guide for the Perplexed, David James
Heidegger: A Guide for the Perplexed, David Cerbone
Hobbes: A Guide for the Perplexed, Stephen J. Finn
Hume: A Guide for the Perplexed, Angela Coventry
Husserl: A Guide for the Perplexed, Matheson Russell
Kant: A Guide for the Perplexed, TK Seung
Kierkegaard: A Guide for the Perplexed, Clare Carlisle
Leibniz: A Guide for the Perplexed, Franklin Perkins
Levinas: A Guide for the Perplexed, B. C. Hutchens
Merleau-Ponty: A Guide for the Perplexed, Eric Matthews
Nietzsche: A Guide for the Perplexed, R. Kevin Hill
Plato: A Guide for the Perplexed, Gerald A. Press
Pragmatism: A Guide for the Perplexed, Robert B. Talisse and Scott F. Aikin
Quine: A Guide for the Perplexed, Gary Kemp
Relativism: A Guide for the Perplexed, Timothy Mosteller
Ricoeur: A Guide for the Perplexed, David Pellauer
Rousseau: A Guide for the Perplexed, Matthew Simpson
Sartre: A Guide for the Perplexed, Gary Cox
Spinoza: A Guide for the Perplexed, Charles Jarrett

THE EMPIRICISTS:
A GUIDE FOR THE PERPLEXED

LAURENCE CARLIN

continuum

Continuum International Publishing Group
The Tower Building   80 Maiden Lane
11 York Road   Suite 704
London   New York
SE1 7NX   NY 10038

www.continuumbooks.com

British Library Cataloguing-in-Publication Data
A catalogue record for this book is available from the British Library.

ISBN-10: HB: 1-8470-6199-0
PB: 1-8470-6200-8
ISBN-13: HB: 978-1-8470-6199-7
PB: 978-1-8470-6200-0

Library of Congress Cataloguing-in-Publication Data
Carlin, Laurence.
The Empiricists : a guide for the perplexed / Laurence Carlin.
p. cm.
Includes bibliographical references.
ISBN-13: 978-1-8470-6199-7 (HB)
ISBN-13: 978-1-8470-6200-0 (pbk.)
ISBN-10: 1-8470-6199-0 (HB)
ISBN-10: 1-8470-6200-8 (pbk.)
1. Empiricism. I. Title.
B816.C37 2009
146′.44–dc22

2008043679

Typeset by Newgen Imaging Systems Pvt Ltd, Chennai, India
Printed and bound in Great Britain by MPG Books Ltd, Bodmin, Cornwall

CONTENTS

CONTENTS

CONTENTS

PREFACE

The purpose of this book is to introduce the philosophical thought of each of the early modern empiricists, and to do so in a way that presents the evolution and culmination of early modern empiricism as a story about great thinkers who shared similar philosophical assumptions. Accordingly, the aims of the book are two, historical and philosophical. The historical aim is to present the views of the seventeenth and eighteenth century empiricists in a way that is sensitive to the intellectual and social context. To this end, Chapter 1 discusses the intellectual context in which these empiricists were working, and subsequent chapters as a whole aim to tell the story of the development of classical empiricism. The philosophical goal is to present the empiricists' philosophical views, and the arguments supporting those views, in a way that would deepen the understanding of the student of philosophy.

The book is primarily intended for those with little or no familiarity with early modern empiricism. While the book is hopefully unique, it does not aim to provide cutting edge research on classical empiricism. Rather, the book aims at a clear presentation of the key thinkers involved in classical empiricism, and a clear presentation of why early modern empiricism is generally regarded a distinctive episode in intellectual history. The book's focus is on two themes that run through all of the classical empiricists. It focuses on each thinker's ontological worldview (what sort of things exist, how those existing things behave, and why they behave the way they do) and on each thinker's views on knowledge and method (what constitutes knowledge of existing things and how we acquire it). Three things are worth noting about the book's approach.

First, due to limitations of space as well as a desire to focus on themes that unite all of the classical empiricists, a number of worthwhile topics were omitted. Perhaps the most glaring omission is Locke's views on personal identity. While this is undoubtedly an important philosophical issue and Locke's discussion is a classic, there already exists a vast literature on the topic. Moreover, it is not directly related to the themes of the book, and one's view of personal identity does not seem to be at the core of what makes one an empiricist – or so it seems to me.

Second, since a goal of the *Guides for the Perplexed* series is to highlight things that students often find perplexing, I have quoted liberally from the texts of the classical empiricists. It seems to me that one of the most challenging things for students of early modern philosophy is to read and penetrate the relevant texts, older texts that contain writing styles alien to our present day writing conventions. Thus, when a significant thesis or argument is being discussed, I tend to incorporate the words of the relevant author – sometimes at length – rather than forcing the reader to rely solely on my words. I hope this will encourage readers to engage the original classic texts too.

Finally, while I quote liberally from the primary sources, I do not at all discuss secondary literature. There are many worthwhile discussions and debates in the secondary literature, and I suggest some of them in the bibliography. But since I have attempted to cover many of the early modern empiricists (instead of merely the usual Locke-Berkeley-Hume trio), limitations of space prevented me from incorporating discussions of secondary literature.

I had a lot of help and support while writing this book. A Faculty Development Grant from the University of Wisconsin Oshkosh supported the project at a crucial juncture. I am grateful for that support.

Thanks are also due to the students of my Cambridge Summer 2008 study abroad programme for making many corrections to the manuscript.

I owe a special thanks to my friend and colleague Marshall Missner for proofreading the entire manuscript, correcting many errors and offering excellent advice throughout. There are still errors, I'm sure, but those are my fault.

My parents, Leo and Kay Carlin, supported my passion for the history of philosophy, and encouraged me to pursue it. They did this knowing that the job prospects for a philosopher were slim. I will always be grateful for their love and encouragement.

My greatest debt is to my wife, Stephanie, and our children, Nathan, Maxwell and Sophie. Their welcome interruptions kept me grounded throughout by reminding me of the most important things in life. This book is dedicated to them with love and gratitude.

Quotations from M. A. Stewart (ed.), *Selected Philosophical Papers of Robert Boyle,* 1991, reprinted by permission of Hackett Publishing Company, Inc. All rights reserved.

References to the works of the empiricists are keyed to the abbreviations in the bibliography.

CHAPTER 1

INTRODUCTION:
THE EMPIRICISTS AND THEIR CONTEXT

1.1. EMPIRICISM AND THE EMPIRICISTS

Empiricism is the view that sensory experience is the source of human ideas (or concepts) and/or human knowledge. The term 'empiricism' does not refer to a precise philosophical position. It is, rather, a type of position with many different applications. One can, for example, be an empiricist with respect to *ideas* by maintaining that all ideas derive from experience, and therefore no ideas are innate. In this latter application, one's empiricism is in large measure a *psychological* theory about how the mind acquires ideas, and how it acquires knowledge.

On the other hand, there is empiricism with respect to the justification of knowledge claims. In this case, one's empiricism is an *epistemological* theory, and according to this theory, sensory experience is the primary justification for knowledge. In this connection, empiricism is usually contrasted with *rationalism,* the view that *reason* (as opposed to sensory experience) is the ultimate justification of our knowledge. But even this distinction between the psychological and epistemological applications of empiricism is crude, for it ignores many differences that can and do exist within each position.

This is not a book about empiricism. It is, as the title indicates, a book about *the empiricists.* One can find empiricists – those who endorse some form of empiricism – throughout the history of philosophy. On some accounts, Aristotle emerged as an empiricist in his criticisms of Plato. In the early twentieth century, many of the founders of analytic philosophy (e.g. A. J. Ayer) saw themselves as empiricists. But the term 'empiricist' is most closely associated with a group of thinkers in the seventeenth and eighteenth centuries. The expression 'classical empiricism' refers to the work of these philosophers. This book is about these classical empiricists. They are:

Francis Bacon (1561–1626)
Thomas Hobbes (1588–1679)
Pierre Gassendi (1592–1679)
Robert Boyle (1627–1691)
John Locke (1632–1704)
Isaac Newton (1642–1727)
George Berkeley (1685–1753)
David Hume (1711–1776)

Usually, only Locke, Berkeley and Hume are counted as the classical empiricists. But as we shall see, there are perfectly good reasons to include all of these thinkers under the rubric of 'classical empiricists'.

If it is true that there are empiricists throughout the history of philosophy, why focus on just these philosophers? There are several reasons but I will mention only two. First, this period is arguably the most tumultuous period in intellectual history, one that contained much controversy. It is during this period, the time of the Scientific Revolution, the post-Reformation and the Enlightenment that the empiricist movement reached heightened proportions, as these philosophers struggled with the radically changing worldview their period produced. As we shall see, this changing worldview made certain important philosophical questions ever more pressing, and this is why focusing on the philosophical doctrines of this historical period is appropriate.

Second, the historical context aside, the philosophers covered in this book were great thinkers who produced philosophical insights of lasting importance. Indeed, it is fair to say that even if there were empiricists prior to these philosophers, no one before them advanced and defended the empiricist movement with such depth and insight. They were brilliant, innovative thinkers, which is why they are considered the 'classic' empiricists. They developed the roots of our own intellectual heritage, and so a close look at their work is of perennial value.

One final point. In the past 20 years or so, scholarship has shown that the labels 'empiricist' and 'rationalist' should be viewed with great caution, for such labels (like many labels in philosophy) can distort and oversimplify. It is true that the thinkers covered in this book privileged sense experience over reason, and that other philosophers of the early modern period (e.g. the rationalists Descartes, Spinoza and Leibniz) privileged reason over sense experience. But it seems that little more than this can be said about the distinction between the empiricists and the rationalists in such broad terms. While each of the philosophers covered in this book were indeed empiricists, there are important differences of approach and outright disagreements between each of them. Also, sometimes a given empiricist's philosophical position bears a striking resemblance to certain rationalist positions. To take one example, Locke, whose empiricist commitments are plain, nonetheless ended up with a theory of knowledge strikingly similar to that of Descartes, one of the leading rationalists of the period. Moreover, there is no evidence that the philosophers of the early modern period viewed themselves as aligned with one team known as 'empiricists' (or 'rationalists'). The distinction is one that was developed by commentators in the centuries following the early modern period.

Still, even though it is difficult to formulate a *precise* non-general philosophical difference between classical empiricism and classical rationalism, that does not mean there is no difference. In one way or another, the thinkers covered in this book privileged sense experience over reason, and rejected the view that united the early modern rationalists: the view that we can have non-empirical rational access to the truth about the world. (e.g. Descartes believed that by beginning with purely rational 'first principles', such as 'I think; therefore, I am', one could proceed to deduce truths about the world, for example, the nature of mind and body.) Each of the thinkers covered in this book denied we can have non-empirical rational access to the truth about the world, and developed a philosophical programme based upon empirical foundations. This book is about these philosophers.

1.2. THE INTELLECTUAL BACKGROUND TO THE EARLY MODERN EMPIRICISTS

The phrase 'modern philosophy' is used by intellectual historians to designate a period when there were radical changes in the way that humans conceived of the world and their place within it. It is generally agreed that this period began sometime around 1600. It is not possible to provide a full treatment in this brief introductory chapter of these radical changes in all their rich detail. Nevertheless, it is crucial to a proper understanding of the empiricists that one bears in mind certain things about their intellectual context. Like any other figures in the history of thought, these philosophers were not writing in a vacuum, but were responding to the issues of their time. To understand these philosophers, we must have some understanding of these contextual issues.

1.2.1. Martin Luther and the Reformation

In 1517, Martin Luther (1483–1546) nailed his famous 95 theses to the door of the church at Wittenburg Castle. These theses were used to express grievances with the Catholic Church. Up until this time, there was *one* Christian Church (the Roman Catholic Church), and it had extensive social and political power. Luther was concerned with what he perceived to be large-scale corruption in the Church, and he was particularly concerned with the monetary sale of indulgences. (An indulgence is a remission of punishment for sins.) Luther campaigned fervently for reform within the Church, but he was excommunicated from the Church in 1521, and he gave up the campaign in favour of setting up a new Church, a Protestant Church. This marked the beginning of the Protestant movement, and led to the establishment of Protestant Churches throughout Europe.

What is significant about this movement for our purposes is that up until the Reformation, it was generally accepted that the Church was the sole authority on spiritual and divine matters, and particularly those having to do with humans' relationship with God and a person's chances for salvation. Luther challenged this authority by insisting that Scripture was the sole authority on such matters, and that salvation was a gift that resulted from faith, a faith unmediated by Church authority.

This entire episode raised fundamental questions in philosophy. For example, what is the relationship between God and the created world? However questions of this sort were answered, this is one example of a general historical shift from a reliance on authority to a reliance on the powers of human reason. We will see in the coming chapters how the empiricists dealt with some of these matters, but more importantly we will see how they too attempted to use reasonable argumentation, as opposed to a reliance on authority.

1.2.2. Aristotelian cosmology and the Scientific Revolution

Just as Church authority traditionally answered religious questions, there were also standard answers to questions in philosophy, and especially in what was known as *natural* philosophy. Natural philosophy is most closely related to what today is known as 'natural science', but in the seventeenth century it included traditional philosophical topics as well. It is a domain of inquiry concerned with every facet of nature, including God's relationship to the natural world, and how one acquires knowledge of that world.

In the thirteenth century, Thomas Aquinas (1225–1274) initiated a powerful synthesis between Christianity and the philosophy of Aristotle – it is sometimes claimed he 'Christianized' Aristotle. This synthesis furthered the cause of *Scholasticism,* a method of learning used widely in schools of the medieval period, and one that usually involved both ancient texts and Catholic theology. All of the empiricists discussed in this book were trained in the medieval Scholastic tradition, and they revolted against this philosophical tradition when framing their philosophies. The Scholastic worldview, rooted in Aristotle and endorsed by the Church, involved certain beliefs about the celestial realm (outer space and its contents), as well as the terrestrial realm of Earth. The former views will be covered first.

The standard view about the celestial realm involved a *geocentric* model of the universe. On the geocentric model, the Earth sat at the centre of the universe in a stationary position, and the sun, stars and every other celestial object revolved around it in perfectly circular motion. The moon, the sun and each of the planets rotated around the Earth on concentric spheres. The outermost sphere was that of the fixed stars, and it rotated on its axis, completing a revolution once every 24 hours. This explained, according to this view, why the stars appeared to rotate around the Earth once every 24 hours. Similar ideas applied to the sun and other celestial bodies. They too were believed to rotate on spheres, as they too appeared to rotate around the Earth once every day. (Witness: we still employ the words 'sun*rise*' and 'sun*set*', though we now know that the sun is not moving relative to the Earth.) There were, of course, many variants of this standard view, and indeed even competing models altogether. But this view, rooted in Aristotle, and presented in his work *On the Heavens* (and developed significantly by the Egyptian astronomer, Ptolemy ca. 83–161 AD), was by far the most common and widely endorsed.

Although religious reasons were not involved in the development of this view, it was eventually seen as fitting well with Christian doctrine: humans were centre stage in the universe not *merely* physically, but also *symbolically*. The Church eventually institutionalized this worldview during the medieval period, as it was congenial to the religious belief that humans have a special place in God's creation. Moreover, variants of this Christian cosmological view maintained that the celestial bodies (the moon, sun, Mars, etc.) were made of different matter than is the Earth, and the matter was increasingly more 'heavenly' the further away it was from Earth. Indeed, most Christians believed that heaven, the place where the angels and blessed lived, was beyond the outermost sphere of the fixed stars.

In short, the common view of the universe was *both* physical and religious, and many saw no distinction between a 'scientific' view of the universe and a religious one. So, when in 1543, Nicolaus Copernicus published his *On the Celestial Revolutions,* it was revolutionary and controversial.

Copernicus offered a different model of the universe, one much closer to the one we have today. According to this familiar model, the Sun is the centre of the universe, and the Earth and other planets revolve around it. Moreover, the Earth, Copernicus explained, has three motions, one of which is a daily rotation, and this is what makes it appear as though the sun is rising and setting. Copernicus' theory was not immediately adopted and indeed, it was initially met with scepticism. But further developments in the years that followed vindicated Copernicus' model. Johannes Kepler (1571–1630) gave us several mathematical laws that captured the elliptical orbiting of Mars around the sun, as well as other laws that explained the varying speeds of planets. Galileo (1564–1642), who was the first to view the celestial realm with a telescope, argued that there were a number of things about the celestial realm that could only be true under the Copernican model and not under the Aristotelian model. Eventually, Isaac Newton would produce the universal theory of gravitation for the planets, thereby closing the door on the old Aristotelian cosmos.

These events mark what has come to be known as 'the Scientific Revolution'. It is difficult to exaggerate the revolutionary significance of this movement. The discovery that the Earth was moving through space like any other planet must stand as one of the most startling discoveries in the history of humanity. Not only did this discovery force humans to rethink the physical spacing and movements of large celestial bodies, but also the discovery overturned what the Church had institutionalized. It now appeared that there was nothing special about humanity's place in the universe, for we are merely inhabitants of one of several planets whirling about the sun. Humans are not 'center stage' and do not occupy a special place in the universe. Moreover, Galileo showed that there is nothing special about the matter in the celestial realm, for it is similar to the matter on Earth and acts with similar motions. These discoveries not only overturned the *physical* aspects of the Aristotelian model, but they seemed to overturn the *religious* aspects of the universe. Indeed, in 1633, Galileo was summoned to the Vatican, and forced to recant his Copernican views.

Just as the Reformation raised philosophical questions about religion, so too the Copernican revolution raised a host of philosophical questions for the empiricists. Perhaps the primary concern that arose had to do with knowledge: what *is* knowledge and how do we know when we have it? For centuries, people thought they knew the correct celestial model. But this turned out to be mistaken, and so questions about the nature of knowledge, the source of knowledge, the extent of knowledge, and the proper method for attaining knowledge, took centre stage for the empiricists.

1.2.3. Aristotelian/Scholastic hylomorphism and the rise of mechanism

The revolutionary discoveries about the celestial realm led to a new way of doing natural philosophy in the terrestrial realm. As noted above, the natural philosophy during the centuries leading up to the modern period was dominated by medieval Scholasticism, and this method of learning was greatly advanced by Aquinas's synthesis of Aristotle and Catholic theology. The empiricists were consciously revolting against this philosophical framework, and in its place offered one based on experimentation and the mathematical properties of matter, for it is upon these foundations that the progress of the Scientific Revolution was based.

The traditional model of natural philosophy prior to the modern period was based on *hylomorphism*. At the most basic level, this is the view that nature consists of individual things – *substances* – each of which is a complex of *matter* and *form*. Matter is the fundamental stuff of which all things are composed. In itself, bare matter has no specific properties, as it is merely the *potential* to become one specific substance or another. Form is what gives matter its specific properties; it is what *actualizes* the potency of matter, makes the substance the thing that it is, and gives it its power to act in a particular way. Usually the form of a substance was understood as something like the shape, or specific arrangement of parts of a given hunk of matter. It is in virtue of the form of a substance (the arrangement of parts) that individual things (an apple, a pen etc.) have their specific properties.

It must be noted that there were many different versions of this Aristotelian hylomorphic framework, and so its specific history is far too rich for detailed coverage here. However, there are three features of this framework that were generally adopted by medieval philosophers, and they are important for understanding the conceptual scheme against which our empiricists were revolting.

First, according to Scholastic hylomorphism, there are two kinds of hylomorphic substances: natural and artificial. Natural substances have an *essential* form to them. The most basic natural substances are the four elements: earth, air, fire and water. Each of these elements has a natural form that determines its properties, and the way it will behave. For example, the form of fire dictates that it will naturally rise, and the form of earth dictates that it will naturally fall. All other inanimate objects have the properties they do because they are composed of different combinations of the elements. So, a rock will naturally fall and not ascend because it is made up primarily of the earth element. Smoke will naturally rise, as it is composed primarily of air and fire. As for animate things, such as humans, they too are natural, and the form of a human, according to Scholastic thought, just is the human soul. Indeed, the human soul became known in the Scholastic tradition as the *substantial form* – a form that 'unifies' the relevant matter (the body), serves as an instigator of growth, and makes the individual an autonomous individual person. On the other hand, artificial substances, such as chairs and tables, do not have their forms naturally. These substances have their forms imposed upon them.

Second, this view of nature came with its own explanatory framework and accompanying method for answering scientific questions ('why' questions). This framework is typically referred to as 'the Four Causes'. Accordingly, a complete explanation of a given thing involves citing four causes: the material cause, the formal cause, the efficient cause, and the final cause. The material cause of a given thing is the matter of which it is composed. The formal cause is the shape or its arrangement of parts. The efficient cause is that which (or whom) produced it, or brought it about. The final cause is the purpose for which it was brought about.

For example, consider the case of an acorn. We can ask a number of 'why' questions – those involved in scientific explanation – about its existence and behaviour, and our answers will appeal to one of these four causes. Why does the acorn fall to the ground? Because the matter (primarily earth element) of which it is composed is heavy (the material cause). Why is the acorn brown and round and have a tendency to grow into an oak tree? Because of the way its matter is arranged (the formal cause). Why does the acorn exist at all? Because it was produced – it grew – from the earth (the efficient cause). Why does the acorn fall from the tree and sprout into the ground? Because it has the natural goal or purpose of becoming a mature oak and reproducing (the final cause).

Notice that a similar explanatory scheme can be provided for artefacts. So, consider a pair of scissors. The material cause is the matter of which it is composed (e.g. metal). The formal cause is the way that matter is arranged. The final cause is the act of cutting, and the efficient cause is the scissors-maker. Typically, the method of producing 'scientific' knowledge was to incorporate such causal explanations into a simple *syllogistic* argument. Consider the following example:

1. All scissors are composed of the earth element. [premise]
2. All things composed of the earth element fall to the ground. [premise]
3. Hence, all scissors fall to the ground. [conclusion]

In this way it was believed that one could produce scientific *knowledge*. The idea here is that if the premises of the syllogism are known (usually they were claimed to be 'self-evident'), then we have an explanation for, and knowledge of the conclusion (3), for the conclusion *must* be true, given the premises. The crucial point for our purposes is that there was almost no emphasis on experimentation, no emphasis on the usefulness of mathematics to science, and the entire method is *deductive* (i.e. it rests on drawing logically certain conclusions from the stipulated premises of a syllogism). Thus, this scientific method is quite foreign to our own, and the empiricists reacted strongly against it.

Finally, the third feature of the Scholastic framework worth highlighting is important in light of the fact that the empiricists placed so much emphasis on sensory perception. According to the hylomorphic tradition, all sensible qualities, such as colours, heat and odours, involve the transmission of a form to the human sensory equipment. Sensory properties were considered real things, and not merely the effects of particles acting on sensory organs. (And they certainly had no conception of colour as a reflection of light waves.) So, when I see a red wall, the quality of red – a form of its own – is received by my senses, and alters the matter that constitutes the eye, forcing me to perceive red. In very broad terms, this was the account of sensory perception for many philosophers. This is important, for as we shall see, one of the central insights of early modern empiricism was that sense perception (again, the root of all knowledge) occurs, *not* by the transmission of forms but by the mechanical impact of invisible particles.

It should be clear that the Scholastic model of nature, like the Aristotelian geocentric model of the universe, meshed well with traditional Christianity. Traditional religious belief maintained that every human being has (or is) a soul, and the doctrine of substantial forms supported this. Christianity also had the view of nature as fundamentally hierarchical, where humans have 'higher' forms (souls) capable of rational thought and religious reflection, which made them candidates for the hereafter. Finally, Scholastic hylomorphism maintained, as we just saw, that nature is fundamentally *teleological,* which means that nature itself is goal-driven, and has definite purposes. (Even the acorn's behaviour is goal driven, and thus subject to final causal explanation.) This fit in well with the larger cosmological view of the time that God's purposes are embedded in the created universe, from the details of the purpose-driven behaviour of acorns, to the stationary centrality of Earth itself.

But all of this came under attack through the work of the early modern empiricists, often under the inspiration of natural philosophers such as Copernicus and Galileo. For a number of reasons, the empiricists (and the rationalists) began to form the belief that this Aristotelian worldview was explanatorily bankrupt. For one thing, the notion of a 'form' was far from clear, for it is not obvious that simply postulating the existence of forms explains anything. For another, Galileo, Kepler and others had shown that a more mathematical approach to nature seems to yield better explanations. And under the leadership of Francis Bacon, most of the empiricists would come to believe that a natural philosophy rooted in *experimentation,* as opposed to the purely theoretical 'syllogistic' method employed by Scholastics, was crucial to understanding nature's ways.

And so the empiricists threw out the hylomorphic model and began campaigning for *mechanism:* the view that all natural change can be explained in terms of the mathematical properties (size, shape, motion) of matter in accordance with laws of nature. Forms were rejected. We shall see the various ways in which each of the empiricists embarked on this transformation, but it should be noted now that this radical change raised a host of philosophical questions: if the world really was merely a conglomerate of matter in motion, where did that motion come from (if not from immaterial forms)? And what shall we say about the place of religious value in a world composed of bits of matter that move in particular ways? How exactly does sense perception, the very vehicle through which we attain knowledge, work? And since we cannot sense all these tiny bits of matter of which the world is composed, just how far does our knowledge of the world extend? These are but a few of the questions that concerned the empiricists. We will engage them in the pages to come.

1.2.4. The Royal Society of London

The final contextual issue worth noting concerns the establishment of societies in Europe for promoting the new natural philosophy. For our purposes, the most important of these was the one established in London in 1660, The Royal Society of London. The Society began somewhat informally with just a few natural philosophers meeting regularly at Gresham College, Oxford, for the purpose of discussing the new natural philosophy, and in particular, the ideas of Francis Bacon (cf. Chapter 2). The official date on which the Society was born was 28 November 1660. There were only 12 initial members, and one of them was Robert Boyle (cf. Chapter 5). Their purpose was to meet regularly, witness scientific experiments, and discuss the new natural philosophy. Eventually, King Charles II learned about the group, and gave them an official Royal Charter in 1662. The Society still thrives today and its fellows are some of the most accomplished scientists in the world. Similar learned societies began to proliferate throughout Europe in places such as Paris, and Berlin.

This government support is significant, for many of the practitioners of the new philosophy were then able to share their ideas and experiments, and present them for peer review. They were also able to publish the findings of some of the members, both in books, and in the journal of the Royal Society, *Philosophical Transactions,* the first issue of which was published in 1665. Several of the thinkers discussed in this book were members of the Royal Society: Robert Boyle, John Locke and Isaac Newton, who became president of the Society in 1703. But even those who were not members benefited indirectly by the development of such societies, for they were established in order to advance the new natural philosophy of the time, and present a united front against the Scholasticism in which they were trained. Indeed, the motto of the Royal Society, *Nullius in verba* (roughly, 'nothing in words') is intended in part to express the Society's rejection of the Scholasticism of the past. The Society's commitment – indeed, the commitment of all the empiricists in this book – was that experience should be the authority, and not merely the 'words' of others. The development of such societies promoted the agenda of all the empiricists, led to optimism with respect to the potential progress of natural philosophy, and in general, provided an impetus for revolutionary intellectual advancement.

It is important to bear in mind in what follows that it is within the intellectual and social context noted above that the empiricists were working. Again, their thoughts were not produced in a vacuum. But by the same token, even though the empiricists were working within a context different from our own, we shall see in the following chapters that many of their insights are of enduring philosophical interest.

CHAPTER 2

FRANCIS BACON (1561–1626)

Francis Bacon was born on 22 January 1561. At the age of 12 he entered Trinity College, University of Cambridge, where he became thoroughly educated in Scholasticism (the merger of Greek philosophy and Catholic theology discussed in Chapter 1). Almost immediately he noticed its deficiencies, and set himself the task of improving the state of natural philosophy in his day. But he also had enormous political ambition, which monopolized much of his time.

His first venture into politics began in 1584 when he was elected to Parliament. He served in Parliament for 37 years. His political career gained significant momentum when James I took the throne, for the previous monarch, Queen Elizabeth I, was not that impressed with Bacon (though she did name him Extraordinary Counsel in 1596). King James knighted Bacon in 1603, and thereafter he quickly ascended the ranks, being named Attorney General in 1613 and Lord Chancellor in 1618. This last position was the highest legal position one could attain, yet Bacon fell from the ranks even more quickly than he ascended them. In 1621, Bacon was charged with accepting bribes while judging cases. Whether the charges were fair is unclear, but in any event Bacon pleaded guilty, admitting that he had accepted gifts from petitioners. (It was pointed out, however, that he decided *against* two such petitioners.) Bacon was fined and spent four days in the Tower of London. Thereafter, he devoted the remainder of his life to his philosophical work and his mission to reform natural philosophy. Unfortunately, he only lived five years after his conviction, and so many of his plans were never completed. Still, he left behind a substantial body of work and his place in the history of great empiricists is secure.

A useful way to approach his empiricism is through his sharp criticisms of the Scholasticism that dominated at the time. His most important work in this connection was *The Great Instauration,* an ambitious work for which Bacon had planned six parts, though he completed only two. What he wrote touched on all of natural philosophy and presented his vision of how one should go about doing natural philosophy. He also pointed out many deficiencies with Scholasticism, but his chief complaint was that the natural philosophy of the time is *stagnant,* for it did not generate new knowledge, but simply rehashed old news.

Bacon did more than criticize, however, for he also made positive contributions by introducing a new method of studying nature that he believed was needed if natural philosophy were to break out of its stagnation. This method, *induction,* is the very method (in a more developed form) used in natural science today, and much of Bacon's legacy derives from his introduction of this method. It involved an emphasis on rigorous empirical observation for collecting data, and in this sense Bacon was not only an empiricist, but also one who would influence several generations of natural philosophers.

But Bacon cautioned that before one can engage in his method of induction, one must prepare the mind to do so. More specifically, one must try to rid the mind of certain preconceptions or inclinations – 'Idols', as Bacon calls them – in order to successfully employ the method. Bacon may very well be more famous for his doctrine of the 'Idols of the Mind' than for anything else. This chapter begins with a discussion of these Idols, and then turns to Bacon's criticisms of Scholastic method, and finally to his own alternative method, one that would prove highly influential.

2.1. THE NATURAL REALM: THE IDOLS OF THE MIND

Even though the doctrine of the Idols is among his most famous contributions, it is often misunderstood and indeed, is often found perplexing. Thus, some discussion of this doctrine is in order, for it is crucial for Bacon's purposes that we understand what these idols are and what they are not.

According to Bacon, the mind is not a blank slate just waiting to absorb, without prejudice, knowledge of nature. Rather, the mind naturally possesses certain inclinations, prejudices or preconceptions that we must acknowledge if we are to do natural philosophy successfully. Bacon calls these preconceptions 'Idols of the Mind', and claims that they 'are the deepest fallacies of the human mind' (WB IV, 431). In his words, they deceive us in our pursuit of truth 'by [way of] a corrupt and ill-ordered predisposition of mind, which as it were perverts and infects all the anticipations of the intellect' (WB IV, 431). They are not 'discriminatory prejudices' as we often use that phrase today (as, for example, when discussing race or class discrimination). Rather, Bacon's idols are tendencies for the mind to misunderstand and become clouded in its quest for knowledge of nature. They are, Bacon believed, a significant part of the natural realm – the mind – and one needs to guard against them.

Bacon wrote in the beginning of his primary philosophical work, *The Great Instauration,* that he believes there are two categories of Idols that plague the human mind: *adventitious* Idols and *innate* Idols (WB IV, 27). Humans are not born with adventitious idols. Rather, such idols infect the mind because of certain kinds of experience. On the other hand, innate idols (as the label suggests) are 'part of the very nature of the intellect' (WB IV, 27), for humans are born with certain psychological propensities that obstruct the successful pursuit of knowledge. Bacon believed there are four types of Idols altogether, two of which are innate, and two of which are adventitious. I discuss each in turn.

2.1.1. Idols of the Tribe

Idols of the Tribe are innately occurring intellectual tendencies that lead one to infer false things. All humans suffer from such idols, as they are part of the very fabric of the human mind in general. They often lead a person to have a distorted image of reality. They stem primarily from the mind's tendency to 'distort and discolour the nature of things by mingling its own nature with it' (WB IV, 54). Bacon believed that humans have an innate tendency to project their own desires for certain views onto nature, regardless of whether nature actually behaves the way that humans want it to. This, of course, is a serious fault, 'for it is a false assertion that the sense of man is the measure of things' (WB IV, 54). As we shall see, Bacon thought there was little hope for completely ridding the mind of its Idols of the Tribe.

He offers several examples of this type of idol at work. First, this idol is manifested when the 'human understanding is of its own nature prone to suppose the existence of more order and regularity in the world than it finds' (WB IV, 55). He cites as an example of this 'the fiction that all celestial bodies move in perfect circles', a clear reference to the Aristotelian cosmology discussed in chapter one. Recall that the standard view of the universe was one according to which Earth was stationary and everything else revolved around it in perfectly circular motion. The human tendency to view the universe in this more 'orderly' and 'regular' way is an example of an idol at work, one that plagued humankind for many years. Bacon's point was that in its quest for knowledge, the mind tends to simplify things by imposing order and regularity where they may not exist.

Second, Bacon pointed out that the human mind, once it has adopted a specific opinion, has a tendency to ignore evidence that tells against it. In this connection, he relayed a parable about a man who was taken into a temple and shown a picture of all those who escaped being shipwrecked after saying their vows to the power of the gods. When he was then asked whether he too acknowledged the power of the gods, he replied thus: 'but where are they painted that were drowned after their vows?' (WB IV, 56). Bacon's point, of course, is that those who showed him the picture were ignoring evidence against their belief in the power of the gods. '[I]t is the peculiar and perpetual error of the human intellect to be more moved and excited by affirmatives than by negatives' (WB IV, 56). Because of the mind's strong desire to be correct, it sometimes ignores evidence against what it holds to be true. And yet, according to Bacon, it should do just the opposite, namely, pay *more* attention to the 'negative' instance: 'Indeed, in the establishment of any true axiom, the negative instance is the more forcible of the two' (WB IV, 56).

There are other examples. Humans tend to be affected by their passionate side: they are impatient, superstitious and overly proud (WB IV, 57). All of this leads them to rush to judgement rather than taking the time required for diligent research. Bacon specifically refers to two aspects of the Scholastic tradition. The first is that because the mind is restless, it presses on 'in vain' to assign reasons to things in general, and,

then it is that in struggling towards that which is further off it falls back upon that which is more nigh at hand; namely, on final causes: which have relation clearly to the nature of man rather than to the nature of the universe; and from this source have strangely defiled philosophy. (WB IV, 57)

In this passage, Bacon associated the pursuit of final causes – a tradition associated with Scholasticism, and discussed in Chapter 1 – with an intellectual idol of the tribe. Specifically, the intellect's tendency to assign reasons and purposes to inanimate things (e.g. acorns) is due to the human tendency to assign its own nature to non-human things. Likewise, he criticized the search for forms (also part of the Scholastic tradition discussed in chapter one) as involving the human tendency to attribute abstract 'figments of the human mind' to nature:

Matter rather than forms should be the object of our attention, its configurations and changes of configuration, and simple action, and law of action or motion; for forms are figments of the human mind. (WB IV, 58)

It was partly Bacon's emphasis on sensory examination on matter, with forms to be rejected, that made him part of the modern empiricist tradition. Although it is human nature to entertain abstract notions, such as forms, the tendency to impute such things to nature is an idol of the tribe.

Finally, 'by far the greatest hindrance and aberration of the human understanding proceeds from the dullness, incompetency, and deceptions of the senses' (WB IV, 58). Our senses do not allow us to perceive the subtle inner workings of matter. They are easily deceived, and prone to accept what appears at first sight. Thus, as we will see, Bacon would go on to encourage careful and methodical empirical research in an attempt to counteract this particular kind of idol.

It is important to bear in mind that Bacon saw all of these examples as involving the human tendency to project its own nature onto the external world. Indeed, it is clear that Bacon viewed the Idols of the Tribe as one of the crucial reasons that natural philosophy had remained stagnant for centuries.

2.1.2. Idols of the Cave

Idols of the Cave are also innate, but they vary according to one's personal innate characteristics. Unlike the Idols of the Tribe this idol can manifest itself differently in different individuals. As Bacon put it, each of us has a 'cave or den of his own':

The Idols of the Cave are the idols of the individual man. For every one (besides the errors common to human nature in general [viz. the Idols of the Tribe]) has a cave or den of his own, which refracts and discolours the light of nature; owing either to his own proper and peculiar nature; or to his education and conversation with others; or to the reading of books, and the authority of those whom he esteems and admires; or to the differences of impressions, accordingly as they take place in a mind. (WB IV 54)

Bacon reported that when it comes to idols of this kind, 'there is a great number and variety' (WB IV, 59). Nonetheless, he did not offer as many examples of these idols as he did for the idols of the tribe. But his general point about them is clear: people possess certain character traits that lead them to be drawn to certain erroneous ways of viewing nature. Certain character traits, when taken in conjunction with one's exposure to certain kinds of education and experiences with others, lead one to form judgements in science and philosophy. These judgements are formed unreflectively, without due attention to nature's actual processes, and at the cost of 'discolouring the light of nature'.

For example, 'men become attached to certain particular sciences and speculations' for the simple reason that they have laboured under them and become habituated to them. In this connection, Bacon mentions Aristotle, 'who made his natural philosophy a mere bond-servant to his logic' (WB IV, 59). That is, Aristotle (and the Scholastics who followed him) had a particular disposition for syllogistic logic and they heavily focused on it, and this determined their entire method by which natural philosophy should be pursued (a method discussed in Chapter 1, and again in the next section of this chapter). Bacon also tells us that some minds are prone to mark distinctions between things in nature, while others are prone to note resemblances. 'Both kinds however easily err in excess' (WB IV, 59). Finally, due to individual character traits, some people are inclined to an extreme admiration of ancient philosophical ways of thinking while others are drawn 'to an extreme love and appetite for novelty' (WB IV, 60). Such blind allegiances can distort one's understanding of nature: 'These factions must be abjured, and care must be taken that the intellect be not hurried by them into assent' (WB IV, 60).

The most important difference between the Idols of the Tribe and the Idols of the Cave is that although they are both innate to the human mind, the Idols of the Cave manifest themselves depending on a given individual's character traits, and the influence that things such as education and society might have upon them. Idols of the Tribe, on the other hand, are similar in the mind of each human. So, although *some* of us are prone to mark excessively distinctions or resemblances in things (an Idol of the Cave), *each* of us is nonetheless inclined to look for more order in nature than is justified (an Idol of the Tribe). But the important similarity between them is that they cannot be avoided, as they are innate propensities of the human mind. All one can do is be aware of their existence, and try not to fall prey to them in excess.

2.1.3. Idols of the Marketplace

The Idols of the Marketplace are not innate. Rather, they are adventitious; that is, they enter the mind because of certain experiences, and once they settle in the human intellect, they become impediments to knowledge. According to Bacon,

> the Idols of the Marketplace are the most troublesome of all: idols which have crept into the understanding through the alliances of words and names. For men believe that their reason governs words; but it is also true that words react on the understanding; and this it is that has rendered philosophy and the sciences sophistical and inactive. (WB IV, 60f.)

Notice that Bacon found these idols 'the most troublesome of all' and blamed them for rendering philosophy and science stagnant. What he had in mind here was the framing of words and definitions based on a faulty understanding of nature, and in particular based on the conception of common people (hence, he calls them idols of the *marketplace,* which is, presumably, a place where the common folk frequent). The problem is that the common vocabulary becomes deeply entrenched, and fixes the understanding on erroneous accounts of the world. This vocabulary of the common folk tends to be indiscriminate in that it does not make distinctions where it should; the language, that is, does not reflect the way that physical nature presents itself (cf. WB IV, 433).

According to Bacon, there are two kinds of idols imposed on the understanding by the ordinary use of words. First, there are words that 'designate' things that simply do not exist. Bacon cited, among other expressions, 'Element of Fire'. The alleged designation of this phrase was discussed in Chapter 1, Section 1.2.3 in connection with Scholastic hylomorphism. Recall that according to that theory the world is composed of four basic natural substances, or 'elements': earth, air, water and fire. As Bacon was increasingly sceptical of hylomorphism, he was also sceptical of the claim that fire is a basic substance of which other things are often composed. There simply is no empirical evidence for such a claim, and so 'element of fire' is an expression that designates something that does not exist (i.e. fire does not exist as a basic element). But Bacon noted that because this type of idol is the result of a faulty theory in natural philosophy, 'it is more easily expelled', for to expunge it from the mind 'it is only necessary that all theories should be steadily rejected and dismissed as obsolete' (WB IV, 61). Bacon, of course, was prepared to wipe the slate clean of the old theories of natural philosophy.

But the second kind of Idol of the Marketplace is not so easily dismissed, since this kind, 'which springs out of a faulty and unskillful abstraction, is intricate and deeply rooted' (WB IV, 61). Bacon was referring here to names of things that seem to exist, but those names are not defined well. Closer analysis, according to Bacon, reveals that such words have no clear meaning (or referent) since they were too hastily defined without careful observation of the entities they are supposed to define. Bacon uses the word 'humid' as an example. At the time, the word had no clear application, and if it was used in one sense, then a certain substance could be called humid, but in another sense that same substance could not be called humid. While Bacon's choice of example may not strike us as relevant today, his general point is clear: people sometimes adopt terminology without having a clear and univocal sense of the meaning of that terminology and that to which it refers. This, Bacon points out, obstructs natural philosophy.

In short, it is Bacon's view that 'the juggleries and charms of words will in many ways seduce and forcibly disturb the judgment' (WB IV, 434). While the first kind of Idol of the Marketplace can be handled by getting rid of false theories (such as Scholastic hylomorphism), the second kind of Idol of the Marketplace 'stand in need of a deeper remedy, and a newer one' (WB IV, 434). Bacon tells us exactly what that remedy is:

[D]efinitions cannot cure this evil [viz. the second kind of market-place idol] in dealing with natural and material things.; since the definitions themselves consist of words, and those words beget others: so that it is necessary to recur to individual instances, and those in due series and order; as I shall say presently when I come to the method and scheme for the formation of notions and axioms. (WB IV, 61)

In this passage, Bacon alluded to his method of induction as a remedy for the idols of the marketplace. This method is discussed in the next section. But first, there is one more idol that needs to be discussed.

2.1.4. Idols of the Theatre

The Idols of the Theatre are nothing other than the received, yet false, theories of natural philosophy. As such, they are clearly not innate, but learned from experience. They are, according to Bacon, mere 'play-books of philosophical systems' with 'perverted rules of demonstration' (WB IV, 62). In general, Bacon identified three kinds of false systems – that is, three kinds of idols of the theatre: 'the Sophistical, the Empirical, and the Superstitious' (WB IV, 64).

The first of these, the Sophistical, is the most important for our purposes, since his target here was the Aristotelianism that dominated in his day. Indeed, Bacon claimed that the 'most conspicuous example of [this] class was Aristotle, who corrupted natural philosophy by his logic' (WB IV, 64). In general, the fault of Aristotelian system-builders (such as the Scholastics) is that they draw on very few instances from experience, and then proceed to generalize on these few instances. That is, the system is insufficiently based (if it is based at all) on experimental observation. It is rooted instead in syllogistic logic and abstract speculation. (Again, we will see more clearly in the next section what Bacon has in mind here.) In a revealing passage, Bacon linked Aristotle and the Scholastics – that is, the 'Schoolmen', as the empiricists often labelled them – in connection with the employment of a false method of learning:

For [Aristotle] had come to his conclusion before; he did not consult experience, as he should have done, in order to the

framing of his decisions and axioms; but having first determined the question according to his will, he then resorts to
experience, and bending her into conformity with his pla-
cets leads her about like a captive in procession; so that even
on this count he is more guilty than his modern followers,
the schoolmen, who have abandoned experience altogether.
(WB IV, 65)

Bacon's chief complaint in connection with the false systems of
natural philosophy was the *methodology* employed within those
systems. He accused Aristotle of 'bending' experience to con-
form to his system. That is, rather than allowing nature to reveal
itself as it actually is, Aristotle interpreted nature falsely in order
to make it fit with his system. His snide remark at the end about
the Scholastics reveals his belief that they followed Aristotle so
uncritically, that they did not even check with experience to see if
Aristotle's system is empirically adequate. This led to a blind allegiance to a false system of natural philosophy, that is, to an Idol
of the Theatre.

The other two kinds of Idols of the Theatre, the Empirical
and the Superstitious, were guilty of somewhat different errors,
according to Bacon. Those from the Empirical school of philosophy, unlike the Aristotelian Sophistical school, did perform
some careful and diligent experiments. But they tended to uni-
versalize the results, suggesting that nature acts everywhere as it
does in this narrowly construed experiment. In this connection,
he mentioned 'the philosophy of [William] Gilbert' (WB IV, 65),
whose rather limited experiments on magnetism led him to formulate an entire system based on the result of that work. Indeed,
Gilbert's hasty expansion of his results is perhaps most evident
in his claim that magnetism is the soul of the Earth. Those who
illegitimately mixed natural philosophy and theology practiced
the Superstitious school of philosophy. In some cases, they
sought explanations in terms of final causes, a topic addressed in
Chapter 1, Section 1.2.3. Bacon cited Plato and his followers as
guilty of utilizing this methodology (though surely Aristotelians
are guilty of it as well). In Bacon's view, science and religion
should not be mixed: 'from this unwholesome mixture of things
human and divine there arises not only a fantastic philosophy but
also a heretical religion' (WB IV, 66).

2.2. KNOWLEDGE AND EXPERIENCE: INDUCTION INTRODUCED

Bacon insisted that the only hope for overcoming the idols is to employ an *inductive* method for the acquisition of knowledge. But overcoming the idols of the mind was not Bacon's only motivation for introducing this new method. On the contrary, he was entirely dissatisfied with the old *deductive* method employed by Scholastic Aristotelians. In order to understand fully Bacon's method and the motivation behind it, it is useful to understand the deductive method of natural philosophy against which he was rebelling.

2.2.1. Aristotelian/Scholastic syllogisms: deductions dismissed

Recall that Bacon accused Aristotle and the Scholastics of drawing on very few instances from experience, and then proceeding to general principles on the basis of these few instances. Bacon had two complaints (among others) about this method: one, it is insufficiently based on experimental observation; two, it is rooted in deductive logic.

The general principle involved in a typical Aristotelian syllogism was based on experience, but only on a few instances. For example, drawing on the Aristotelian theory of elements, we can see that the Scholastics would take the following to be a scientific principle:

(1) All objects composed primarily of the earth element naturally descend.

This principle stood as a generalization from a few casually observed instances of 'earth stuff'. On the basis of such a principle, one could then form deductive inferences. That is, one could reason *from* this general truth *to* a particular instance. For example:

(1) All objects composed primarily of the earth element naturally descend.
(2) This book is composed primarily of the earth element.
(3) Hence, this book naturally descends.

What makes this a *deductive* inference is that it proceeds from the principle to particular instances, and does so in a way that makes the conclusion follow *necessarily* from the premises: given the truth of the premises (1) and (2), the conclusion (3) *must* be true.

As odd as it may seem to us, this method was understood to be the paradigm for scientific knowledge in the Aristotelian/Scholastic tradition, for it was held that since the general principle is true, it explains the fact (3) to be established, and does so with certainty.

Bacon was particularly unsatisfied with this aspect of Scholasticism, and he launched several criticisms against it. For example, as noted above, it proceeds very quickly from a limited number of observations – observations not grounded in rigorous experiment – to generalizations. This, of course, is a suspicious move. Second, the method offers no way for telling us what a given substance *is:* what exactly is the 'earth element'? As we shall see, he believed his new method could answer such questions. Finally, the method leaves no room for new scientific knowledge. We have seen above that Bacon lamented the fact that the natural philosophy of his time was stagnant. Here we see partly what was to blame, for the deductive method left no room for progress since the conclusion (that which is to be explained) was already basically contained in the premises (1) and (2). How then could one make progress with respect to knowledge of the natural world? Bacon's answer to this question, along with his criticism of the syllogistic method is found early on in *The Great Instauration:*

> The syllogism consists of propositions, propositions consist of words, words are symbols of notions. Therefore if the notions themselves (which is the root of the matter) are confused and over-hastily abstracted from the facts, there can be no firmness in the superstructure. Our only hope therefore lies in true induction. (WB IV, 49)

The only way to make progress is to pay closer attention to physical nature to avoid faulty concepts of nature, a way that demands 'true induction'.

2.2.2. Baconian empiricism: induction introduced

Bacon believed that unlike the deductive Aristotelian method, his new method was one that is firmly grounded in experimental observation, as well as one that allows for the growth of new knowledge.

Contemporary scientific method has its historical roots in Bacon's method of induction, though it is not identical with it. For Bacon, one must assemble 'tables' of 'instances' of the entity or process under investigation. When these tables are complete, one is then in a position to do induction:

> The work and edifice of these three tables I call the Presentation of Instances to the Understanding. Which presentation having been made, Induction itself must be set to work; for the problem is, upon a review of the instances, all and each, to find such a nature as is always present or absent with the given nature, and always increases and decreases with it; and which is, as I have said, a particular case of a more general nature. (WB IV, 145)

Bacon indicated in this passage that the goal is to find a specific 'nature' that correlates with ('is present or absent with') the thing under investigation ('the given nature'). This is the goal to be attained from the creation of the tables. When this is complete, we turn to induction, and the goal of induction is to find specific 'forms' of things – but it *must* be emphasized that he did *not* have in mind the traditional Scholastic notion of form discussed in Chapter 1. Indeed, Bacon wrote that he 'cannot too often warn and admonish men against applying what [he] says to those forms to which their thoughts and contemplations have hitherto been accustomed' (WB IV, 146). Rather, when Bacon wrote that we ought to search for forms, he seems to have meant that we ought to try to identify the internal constitution of nature's objects in such a way that we would have an explanation of all of that object's properties. It must be admitted, however, that many scholars have found Bacon's characterization of forms unclear. But as we are about to see by way of Bacon's favourite example, his discussion suggests something like this interpretation.

Notice that in the passage quoted above, Bacon wrote that preparatory to the practice of induction, one must assemble *three* tables, which together he called the 'Presentation of Instances to the Understanding'. More specifically, Bacon believed that we must assemble what he calls three 'Tables and Arrangements of Instances' (WB IV, 127). The idea behind this arrangement is to isolate those natures or properties that are always found with (and never found without) the thing under investigation. Bacon's favourite example consisted of an investigation into 'the Form of Heat' (WB IV, 127ff.), and he drew up three tables involving extensive observations about the presence and absence of heat in various situations. The three tables are appropriately labelled:

(1) Table of Essence and Presence
(2) Table of Deviation, or of Absence in Proximity
(3) Table of Degrees or Comparison in Heat

In the first table, Bacon offered a list of 'instances agreeing in heat', or in other words, examples of cases in which heat is present. His list is extensive and contains examples such as 'the rays of the sun', 'liquids boiled or heated', and 'horse-dung and like excrements of animals when fresh' (WB IV, 128).

In the second table, Bacon offered a list of 'instances in proximity where the nature of heat is absent', or in other words, examples of things and processes that do not involve heat. Obviously, this list could go on indefinitely, so Bacon suggested that we limit it to the cases 'most akin' to the cases in the first table. So, as an example of an absence of heat akin to the rays of the sun, Bacon listed the rays of the moon, which he believed are not hot (WB IV, 129). (He was, of course, wrong about this, for there is indeed reflected solar heat in the moon's rays.) As an example of an absence of heat akin to heated liquids, Bacon listed 'liquid itself in its natural state', and noted that the warmth of liquids is temporary, as liquids tend to cool, and are never found naturally to remain hot (WB IV, 133). He did not think there was a negative instance akin to the case of horse-dung.

Finally, the third table contains examples in which heat is found in different degrees, 'which must be done by making a comparison either of its increase and decrease in the same subject, or its amount in different subjects, as compared one with another' (WB IV, 137). For example, Bacon noted that some substances become hotter than flames, as iron does when it is heated. He also noted that when animals exercise, they become hotter. These sorts of cases document not simply the presence or absence heat, but its increase and diminution.

The assumption behind the construction of these tables is that it will now be possible though not easy, to rule out, on the basis of the information supplied by these tables, certain natures (or properties) not involved in the ultimate form of heat. It is at this point that we are engaged in induction:

The first work therefore of true induction (as far as the discovery of Forms) is the rejection or exclusion of the several natures which are not found in some instance where the given nature is present, or are found in some instance where the given nature is absent, or are found to increase in some instance when the given nature decreases, or to decrease when the given nature increases. Then indeed after the rejection and exclusion has been duly made, there will remain at the bottom, all light opinions vanishing into smoke, a Form affirmative, solid and true and well defined. (WB IV, 145f.)

Although Bacon's writing here is perhaps a bit rough for the contemporary reader, a careful examination of the passage reveals the central point: we must eliminate those cases in which heat is present, but some other 'instance' is not involved. For example, we can rule out that light is involved in the form of heat because the moon's rays are not hot (or so Bacon believed). We can also rule out, Bacon argued, that any one kind of bodily texture is involved in heat, since so many kinds of bodies acquire heat (minerals, animals, vegetables, water, air, etc.). In the end, Bacon wrote in the passage above, we arrive at the true form of heat. That is, we will have isolated that characteristic of heat that is always present, and never absent.

To the extent that we cannot rule out, on the basis of the tables, a given hypothesis concerning the form of heat, our hypothesis is confirmed. We are then in a position, according to Bacon, to put forward the true form of heat: 'heat is a motion, expansive, restrained and acting in its strife upon the smaller particles of bodies' (WB IV, 154). We can likewise lay down some law-like generalizations on the basis of our discovery: 'while it expands all ways, it has at the same time an inclination upwards', and 'it is not sluggish, but hurried and with violence' (WB IV, 154f.). (It is worth noting in passing that Bacon's remarks about the nature of heat were not too far from our contemporary understanding of the nature of heat.) Again, to the extent that we cannot provide, on the basis of experimental observation as reported in our tables, a counterexample to these discoveries, they are to that very extent confirmed. As Bacon noted, this is precisely what makes 'negative instances' (counter-examples) so important: 'Indeed, in the establishment of any true axiom, the negative instance is the more forcible of the two' (WB IV, 56).

There are two features of this method that must be emphasized for our purposes. First, the method demands *extensive* and detailed empirical observation for the gathering of knowledge. This is something that was not emphasized before Bacon, and so it is revolutionary in this respect. Second, the way of reasoning involved in induction is such that, unlike the deductive method used in the Aristotelian tradition, any conclusions drawn are not guaranteed. Leaving aside Bacon's extensive tables, and updating his method a bit, we might simplify his way of reasoning above in the following way:

(1) Observed instance a of heat involved properties xyz.
(2) Observed instance b of heat involved properties xyz.
(3) Observed instance c of heat involved properties xyz.

And so on . . . .. Therefore, *all* instances of heat involve properties xyz.

As laid out, this is an *inductive argument*: the conclusion generalizes that an *entire* class of instances will resemble those sorts of instances one has observed in the past. Clearly, this reasoning is not immune to error, for it is always possible that the conclusion is false despite the truth of the premises involving past observations. Nonetheless, if we believe that one of the aims of science is to reveal the law-like generalizations that obtain in nature, this is the proper way of getting at them, for it proceeds from a rigorous study of the particulars of nature to a generalization of how nature works. This, of course, is how science has proceeded for the last few centuries, and largely thanks to Bacon's method, it has been remarkably successful.

2.3. CONCLUSION: BACON THE EMPIRICIST

Bacon's place in the history of natural philosophy is secure, for his method of induction influenced centuries of scientific research. But what is it exactly that makes Bacon an empiricist?

Bacon is a classic empiricist certainly because of his insistence that knowledge of the world is rooted in sensory observation. He might also be classified an empiricist because he realized that many of the innate tendencies of the human mind – the idols – are not to be trusted. Rather, one should trust *experience,* or what nature 'tells' the mind. It is true that Bacon did not develop a full-blown epistemological theory of the sort we find in Locke (cf. Chapter 6). But he provided the sort of empirical method that subsequent epistemologists (such as Locke) attempted to justify with their empiricist theories of knowledge. This clearly suffices to show that Bacon was a part of the empiricist camp, and in any event, subsequent empiricists saw themselves as part of a way of thinking that was started by Bacon. He drew our attention to the habits and inclinations of the mind, and a more fruitful way of directing the mind in the search for knowledge. These themes will emerge again in subsequent chapters.

CHAPTER 3

THOMAS HOBBES (1588–1679)

Thomas Hobbes was born on 15 April 1588 on the outskirts of Malmesbury, England. At the age of 20 (1608), he graduated from Magdalen College, Oxford University, where he was thoroughly educated in scholastic thought. Like all of the classic empiricists, he was highly critical of scholasticism, which according to him frequently used 'insignificant speech' (EW 3, 3). Indeed, at one point, Hobbes stated bluntly that 'scarce anything can be more absurdly said in natural philosophy, than that which is now called *Aristotle's Metaphysics*' (EW 3, 669). Hobbes preferred to immerse himself in the new natural philosophies of the seventeenth century.

Shortly after completing his university studies, Hobbes found work as a tutor to the son of William Cavendish. This proved to be quite an opportunity, for not only did it permit him to talk often with Francis Bacon (for whom he did some secretarial work), it also enabled him to travel throughout Europe and meet some of the leading intellectuals on the Continent, including Pierre Gassendi (Chapter 4) and Galileo. His association with the Cavendish family made him somewhat famous. It also put him squarely on the side of royalty during the English civil war, and he published defences of royal sovereignty.

He was also famous (especially in England) for his open controversies with leading figures of the time. In 1645 he engaged in a public debate with Bishop John Bramhall about the nature of free will. In 1662, Robert Boyle (Chapter 5) established the influential Royal Society of London (Chapter 1, Section 1.2.4), and Hobbes was not invited to be a member. Though it is not clear why he was not invited, it was probably because he was suspected of being an atheist. In any event, Hobbes would later enter into a very public dispute with Boyle about the importance of experimentation in science, among other issues. He also engaged in an intense debate with the English mathematician John Wallis over Hobbes's claim in 1655 to have 'squared the circle'. That is, Hobbes claimed to have constructed a square equal in area to a given circle. He was wrong.

Up until his travels throughout Europe, Hobbes was mostly interested in classics, and indeed he published translations of classical works. But this immersion into the scientific community on the Continent made his interest in philosophy grow. Beginning in the 1640s, Hobbes began publishing a number of works in philosophy, and especially in political philosophy, for which he is most famous. His *magnum opus, Leviathan* (1651) is a classic in the history of political philosophy, though we shall not cover his political theory here. It is an enormous work in which Hobbes attempted to demonstrate the need for an absolute political sovereign based on mechanical and psychological facts about human beings. Though now regarded a classic, at the time it earned him the nickname 'Monster of Malmesbury', for it was widely read as having atheistic implications, as well as sympathy for the monarchy during the English Revolution, and this of course enraged Parliamentarians.

In addition to the *Leviathan,* Hobbes's most important work for our purposes is the *Elements of Philosophy.* It consists of three volumes, each published separately: *De Cive* ('On the Citizen'; 1642), *De Corpore* ('On Body'; 1655) and *De Homine* ('On Man', 1658). Together these three volumes address everything from the politics of civil society, to the psychology of human beings, to the nature and principles of motion. Throughout all of these works, Hobbes made his rejection of Scholasticism abundantly clear. In its place, he offered a mechanistic worldview rooted in a commitment to materialism. He also offered a scientific methodology radically different from Bacon's that did not have much influence. Still, it is worth a look, since it is a particularly clear example of how the scientific method we often take for granted today was not so obviously the correct one from the viewpoint of the classical empiricists, but one that evolved gradually during the early modern period.

3.1. THE NATURAL REALM: HOBBES'S MATERIALISTIC MECHANISM

Hobbes was a *materialist*. That is, he believed that the only thing that exists is matter. This entails that immaterial substances, such as human souls, do not exist, as many in the seventeenth century believed (including some other empiricists). Hobbes was convinced that each existing thing – including each human being – is just a hunk of matter in motion. Some of these pieces of matter are imperceptibly small, and some are quite large. Some hunks of matter behave in certain ways that others do not. But Hobbes's fundamental conviction was that the universe contains nothing but matter. Moreover, there is matter *everywhere*. That is, Hobbes was a *plenist*, for he did not believe there could be a vacuum, or space devoid of matter.

More specifically, the Hobbesian world is one of matter *in motion*. His understanding of philosophy as a discipline was consistent with his conviction that the universe consists fundamentally of matter in motion:

Philosophy *is such knowledge of effects or appearances, as we acquire by true ratiocination from the knowledge we have first of their causes or generation; and again, [knowledge] of such causes or generations as may be from knowing first their effects.* (EW 1, 3)

For Hobbes, philosophy is about using 'ratiocination' to discover causal relations. His conception of 'true ratiocination' is discussed in the next section, but we may think of it for now merely as a form of proper reasoning. When his definition of philosophy is considered in conjunction with his materialism, this means that philosophy is about discovering how the motions of matter cause other states of matter in motion. It is difficult to exaggerate the importance of motion for Hobbes, for in the dedicatory letter of *De Corpore*, Hobbes claimed that Galileo 'was the first that opened to us the gate of natural philosophy universal, which is the knowledge of the nature of *motion*' (EW 1, viii). Hobbes believed that, in theory at least, matter in motion could explain every facet of the world.

3.1.1. The importance of motion

According to Hobbes, any hunk of matter – that is, any 'body' – '*is that, which having no dependence on our thought, is coincident or coextended with some part of space*' (EW 1, 102). That is, a body is something that occupies space and has length, breadth and depth. Any existing body will, of course, be in a specific *place*, and Hobbes defined place as '*that space which is possessed or filled adequately by some body'* (EW 1, 70). Consistent with these definitions, Hobbes defined motion thus: 'motion *is a continual relinquishing of one place, and acquiring of another'* (EW 1, 109). And motion is the most basic universal cause involved in all natural changes (cf. EW 7, 83):

> But the causes of universal things . . . are manifest of themselves, or (as they say commonly) known to nature; so that they need no method at all; for they have all but one universal cause, which is motion. For the variety of all figures arises out of the variety of those motions by which they are made; and motion cannot be understood to have any other cause but motion; nor has the variety of those things we perceive by sense, as of *colours, sounds, savours,* etc. any other cause than motion, residing partly in the objects that work upon our senses, and partly in ourselves, in such manner, as that it is manifestly some kind of motion. (EW 1, 69f.; cf. EW 7, 83)

By 'universal things', Hobbes meant such properties that are common to all bodies, and he claimed in this passage that the motion of bodies can explain everything. Moreover, motion, as an explanatory principle, is self-evident, or 'manifest in itself', such that it needs no further explanation; it needs no further 'method' of analysis. It is the fundamental basis of all causal analysis. This is a significant claim for our purposes, as we will that other empiricists believed that motion, or the source of motion, *did* require an explanation. This topic will loom large in the coming chapters.

Hobbes also claimed in the passage above that sense perception occurs *via* matter in motion. His materialist account of sense perception is discussed below, but some general preliminaries about his understanding of motion as a causal agent are in order.

Hobbes was an unrelenting mechanist. Recall from Chapter 1, Section 1.2.3 that mechanism is the view that all natural change is to be explained in terms of mathematical properties (size, shape, motion) of matter in accordance with laws of nature. As a mechanist, he believed that there are restrictions on what could count as an intelligible explanation of the behaviour of bodies. For example, Hobbes maintained that no body can move itself, for the only way a body could be moved is by another body in motion that comes into contact with it. Likewise, any body in motion will remain in motion unless it comes in contact with another body (cf. EW 1, 124f., 205).

The restriction that all natural change must occur through mechanical impact implied for Hobbes that there could not be *action at a distance*. The notion of action at a distance was problematic for nearly all early modern philosophers. It was part of the mechanical way of thinking that any body that interacted with another must do so through contact. But some causal relations might seem to occur over a spatial distance, not through mutual contact. The most perspicuous case for our purposes is that of gravity: the Earth seems to cause heavy objects to fall to Earth, even though the relevant heavy object was not in contact with the Earth. This problem will be discussed in greater detail in Chapter 7 when Newton is covered (cf. Chapter 7, Section 7.1.3). It suffices for now to note that Hobbes found action at a distance unintelligible, and thus any apparent case of action at a distance must be explained by appeal to imperceptible intervening bodies that transmit the causal influence – that is, imperceptible particles of matter between the heavy object and the Earth. (For Hobbes's attempt to explain gravity in this way, see EW 1, 511ff.) It is partly for this reason that Hobbes was a plenist, for a plenist could claim that such intervening bodies are everywhere available to transmit causal influence.

Hobbes's allegiance to a mechanical worldview where the concept of motion stood centre stage also led him to reject the Scholastic model of explanation (discussed in Chapter 1, Section 1.2.3), according to which there are four causes. For Hobbes, there are efficient causes, and they are states of matter in motion that produce other states of matter in motion. Although he sometimes mentioned the other Scholastic causes, he seems to have believed that they were all reducible to efficient causal states of matter.

There is one more crucial element of Hobbes's views on motion for our purposes. Just as he employed the concept of a universe that consists of tiny undivided and imperceptible parts of matter, so too he made use of the idea of tiny imperceptible bits of motion that he called 'endeavours':

I define ENDEAVOUR *to be motion made in less space and time than can be given;* that is, *less than can be determined or assigned by exposition or number;* that is, *motion made through the length of a point, and in an instant or point of time.* (EW 1, 206)

The notion of 'endeavour' ('*conatus*' in Latin) is abstract, to say the least. It suggests a kind of 'effort' involved in motion, a striving from one place to another. But at the same time, Hobbes claims that it *is* motion, which he understood to be a body's transference from one place to another. The relevant transference takes place in an imperceptible amount of time and space. However it is to be understood, the reasoning that led him to the notion of endeavour seems clear enough:

And although unstudied men do not conceive any motion at all to be there, where the thing moved is invisible; or the space it is moved in is, for the shortness of it, insensible; yet that doth not hinder, but that such motions are. For let a space be never so little, that which is moved over a greater space, whereof that little one is part, must first be moved over that. These small beginnings of motion . . . are commonly called ENDEAVOUR. (EW 3, 39)

The reasoning is this: any body that moves through a given amount of space must travel through the imperceptible parts of that space. And the motion required to travel through these tiny bits of space – bits smaller than can be assigned – are themselves tiny bits of motion, that is, endeavours.

The notion of endeavour played an important role in Hobbes's philosophy, as he used it to define and explain a number of things. For our purposes, the most important application is the role it played in his account of sense perception.

3.1.2. Sensation and the mind

Hobbes is an empiricist in large part because of his insistence that the 'first beginnings . . . of knowledge, are the phantasms of sense and imagination' (EW 1, 66). By 'phantasm', Hobbes meant a sensible or mental image, and what later empiricists (and occasionally Hobbes) simply called an 'idea', or that which appears to the sensing mind. With respect to such appearances,

[t]he original of them all, is that which we call SENSE, for there is no conception in a man's mind, which hath not at first, totally, or by parts, been begotten upon the organs of sense. The rest are derived from that original. (EW 7, 1; cf. EW 1, 411)

This passage is from the opening paragraphs of *Leviathan,* and it is passages of this sort that lead one to classify Hobbes as an empiricist, for here he flatly stated one of the principal empiricist theses: all ideas derive from sensory experience.

Recall that Hobbes defined philosophy as involving in part knowledge of *'such causes or generations as may be from knowing first their effects or appearances'* (EW 1, 387; cf. EW 1, 3). Given that sense perception is the origin of knowledge and that we must start with what we 'know' – that which 'appears' to the senses – it is natural that Hobbes would hold that 'in the first place, therefore, the causes of our perception, that is, the causes of those ideas and phantasms which are perpetually generated within us whilst we make use of our senses, are to be enquired into; and in what manner their generation proceeds' (EW 1, 389). His understanding of philosophy is in accordance with this procedure: if philosophy involves the inquiry into the causes of things that appear, then the cause of the items of sense perception is the starting point for learning *how* humans gain knowledge of the materialistic, mechanistic, and deterministic world.

Not surprisingly, Hobbes reduced sense perception to states of matter in motion: 'Sense, therefore, in the sentient, can be nothing else but motion in some of the internal parts of the sentient; and the parts so moved are parts of the organs of sense' (EW 1, 390). We noted in the last section that Hobbes believed all natural change must occur through mechanical impact, or by way of contiguous states of matter impacting each other. He explicitly adhered to this view when it came to his account of sense perception: 'I have shown . . . that no motion is generated but by a body contiguous and moved: from whence it is manifest, that the immediate cause of sense or perception consists in this, that the first organ of sense is touched and pressed' (EW 1, 390; cf. EW 3, 1). So, Hobbes's view was that any perceptual process begins by having one's sense organs causally impacted ('touched and pressed') by material particles. His task was to explain exactly how this worked, and indeed he provided quite a bit of detail. But in the end, there is reason to believe that even he was not fully confident that he had the right account.

The most detailed explanation of how sense perception works is found in *De Corpore* (though a 'briefer' account can be found in the opening chapters of *Leviathan;* see EW 3, 1f.):

For when the uttermost part of the organ is pressed, it no sooner yields, but the part next within it is pressed also; and, in this manner, the pressure or motion is propagated through all the parts of the organ to the innermost. And thus also the pressure of the uttermost part proceeds from the pressure of some more remote body, and so continually, till we come to that from which, as from its fountain, we derive the phantasm or idea that is made in us by our sense. And this, whatsoever it be, is that we commonly call *the object*. Sense, therefore, is some internal motion in the sentient, generated by some internal motion of the parts of the object, and propagated through all the media to the innermost part of the organ. By which words I have almost defined what sense is. (EW 1, 390f.)

In this passage, we get a somewhat graphic picture of what Hobbes has in mind. Upon perceiving a certain object, many imperceptible bits of matter impact ('press') the outer ('uttermost') surface of the relevant sensory organ. These bits of matter were in turn impacted by other bits of matter that are closer to the relevant object, and these bits of matter were impacted by other bits of matter that are even closer to the relevant object, and so on. We can trace this chain of mechanical impacts to the object itself. So, in the end, the object impacts my sense organ *via* states of imperceptible bits of matter in motion. When the sense organ is impacted, in turn, the surface particles of my sense organ impact the inner particles that make up my sense organ, which in turn impact further inner particles of my sense organ, and so on, until this causal process results in a phantasm, or an appearance of the relevant object.

Note that Hobbes concluded the above passage by writing that he has '*almost* defined what sense is'. Indeed, there is more to his account, and it is at this point that his notion of endeavour plays a crucial role:

Moreover, I have shown that all resistance is endeavour opposite to another endeavour, that is to say, reaction. Seeing, therefore, there is in the whole organ, by reason of its own internal natural motion, some resistance or reaction against the motion which is propagated from the object to the innermost part of the organ, there is also in the same organ an endeavour opposite to the endeavour which proceeds from the object; so that when that endeavour inwards is the last action in the act of sense, then from the reaction, how little soever the duration of it be, a phantasm or idea hath its being; which, by reason that the endeavour is now outwards, doth always appear as something quite situate without the organ. (EW 1, 391; cf. EW 3, 2)

Hobbes's point seems to be this: the sensory organs, upon impact by those imperceptible bits of matter in motion involved in sense perception, exhibit a resistance to that impact. This resistance consists in endeavour, instantaneous strivings of motion *against* those bits of matter impacting the sensory organs. And when the last bit of resistance or endeavour occurs in the 'innermost part of the organ', it creates a sensory image – a 'phantasm or idea'. But moreover – and this appears to be an important function of endeavour – the resistance or endeavour given by the inner parts of the sensory organs, an endeavour 'outwards', makes it appear as though the object of perception exists outside of us, even though the idea, phantasm, or appearance of it does not exist outside of us, for the phantasm is a mental entity (a sensible image), and as such, exists inside the head.

With the incorporation of the role of endeavour, Hobbes believed he was now in position to give us a definition of 'sense':

So that now I shall give you the whole definition of sense, as it is drawn from the explication of the causes thereof and the order of its generation, thus: SENSE *is a phantasm, made by the reaction and endeavour outwards in the organ of sense, caused by an endeavour inwards from the object, remaining for some time more or less.* (EW 1, 391)

In light of the preceding paragraphs, one can see now why Hobbes defines 'sense' in this way. In this full-blown definition, one can see how much weight he was prepared to put on the notion of endeavour when it came to sensation.

Hobbes's account is perplexing. It is not at all clear how accumulations of matter in motion can give rise to, or be identical to a sensible image of, say, a zebra. After all, sensible images in themselves do not seem to *be* material items, for a set of imperceptible bits of matter in motion is one thing, and a sensible image is another. One might argue that the former does not have the 'feel' of a sensible image of a zebra, or the qualitative feel of hearing an orchestra or smelling a rose. Moreover, it is not clear why certain bits of matter should be identical to one sensible experience (a visual perception of a zebra) as opposed to another (an auditory experience of an orchestra). What makes one accumulation of matter 'zebra-like', while another accumulation 'orchestra-like'? The answer, presumably, has to do with the mathematical properties (size, shape, motion) of the relevant bits of matter. But it is far from clear why this alone should make for such an enormous qualitative difference.

Nor is it clear how the endeavour involved in sense perception leads one to believe that the zebra exists at a spatial distance from the perceiver, let alone at a *specific* spatial distance. In general, Hobbes had little evidence for the account he offered. It would appear instead to be grounded in the firm conviction he had (discussed in the previous section) that the world was fundamentally mechanical and all natural change was nothing more than matter in motion. While one might be sympathetic to this attempt to 'mathematize' nature in the midst of the rejection of Scholastic thought, it must also be admitted that Hobbes's account of sensation is far from bulletproof. (It is worth noting in passing that many contemporary accounts of sense perception also reduce sensations to matter in motion, and are also often just as puzzling.)

But having noted these perplexing features of the account, we should also note that Hobbes prefaced the entire account in *De Corpore* with the following remarks:

I now enter upon the other part; which is the finding out by the appearances or effects of nature, which we know by sense, some ways and means by which they *may* be, *I do not say they are,* generated. The principles, therefore, upon which the following discourse depends, are not such as we ourselves make and pronounce in general terms, as definitions . . . [n]or do they impose upon us any necessity of constituting theorems; their use being only . . . to show us the *possibility* of some production or generation. (EW 1, 388; my emphasis)

To be fair, Hobbes indicated in this passage that he believed his account of sensation to be at least partly speculative, for he did not, as he wrote above, purport to be giving a definitive or even likely account, but only a 'possible' one. As we shall see in the next section, his hesitation here was a result of his views on the very nature and methodology of natural philosophy. Still, given how much he wrote about it in *De Corpore* and *Leviathan* and other places, he must have had some confidence in it. And as we shall see, he was not entirely alone, for other empiricists offered an account of sensation along similar mechanistic lines.

But whatever the problems with Hobbes's account of sensation, it is interesting in that it shows a systematic unity to his philosophy. It is remarkably consistent with his views on motion and causation, and indeed his mechanical outlook in general. Hobbes's desire for systematic unity is equally clear in his account of imagination:

> When a body is once in motion, it moveth, unless something else hinder it, eternally; and whatsoever hindreth it, cannot in an instant, but in time, and by degrees, quite extinguish it; and as we see in the water, though the wind cease, the waves give not over rolling for a long time after: so also it happeneth in that motion, which is made in the internal parts of a man, then, when he sees, dreams, etc. For after the object is removed, or the eye shut, we still retain an image of the thing seen, though more obscure than when we see it. . . . IMAGINATION therefore is nothing but *decaying sense;* and is found in men, and many other living creatures, as well sleeping, as waking. (EW 3, 4f.)

In this passage, Hobbes appealed to one of his mechanical commitments discussed in the last section, viz., the view that any body in motion will remain in motion unless it comes in contact with another body (cf. EW 1, 124f., 205). It is clear from this passage that this latter view motivated his account of imagination. Just as ripples in water continue to move for some time despite no longer having the wind behind them, so too the motion that occurs during sense perception does not halt all at once, but 'decays' slowly. This 'decaying' motion *just is* imagination, or the less vivid sensible images involved in memory and imagination.

As an empiricist, he was committed to the view that all ideas derive from sensory experience. Present sensory experience occurs *via* matter in motion. Thus, acts of imagination and memory, in virtue of being derived from previous sensory experiences, are the decaying results of those previous states of matter in motion. Here again, we see a systematic unity in Hobbes's philosophy, and indeed he also sought to explain other mental operations (e.g. desire, pleasure etc.)

in terms of his materialist and mechanistic commitments. (These other accounts are beyond the scope of this book.)

But Hobbes did not believe that merely having sensory experience was sufficient to secure very much *knowledge* about that which one experienced. In order to obtain such knowledge, one needs the proper method for reasoning with the ideas of sense experience. Hobbes believed that Euclid provided that method.

3.2. KNOWLEDGE AND EXPERIENCE: DEFINITIONS AND THE EUCLIDEAN METHOD

Recall that in *De Corpore,* Hobbes remarked that he was not giving a definitive account of sense perception, but only a 'possible' one (EW 1, 388). His reluctance here is part of a general tendency in his thought about the method of natural philosophy and the kind of knowledge it could yield, for Hobbes did not believe that natural philosophy could yield perfect certainty. Thus, our knowledge of nature's processes can never attain more than a probabilistic certainty, and must always remain hypothetical in nature. This is a substantial epistemological conclusion, and it is worth investigating what led Hobbes to it.

3.2.1. Two kinds of knowledge and proper ratiocination

According to Hobbes, there are two kinds of knowledge:

> There are of knowledge two kinds; whereof one is *knowledge of fact;* the other *knowledge of the consequence of one affirmation to another.* The former is nothing else, but sense and memory, and is *absolute knowledge;* as when we see a fact doing, or remember it done: and this is the knowledge required in a witness. The latter is called *science;* and is *conditional;* as when we know, that, *if the figure shown be a circle, then any straight line through the centre shall divide it into two equal parts.* And this is the knowledge required in a philosopher; that is to say, of him that pretended to reasoning. (EW 3, 71)

Hobbes here drew a distinction between 'knowledge of fact' and 'knowledge of the consequence of one affirmation to another'. (We shall call this latter type, *conditional knowledge.*) The former amounts to nothing more than knowledge of the contents of sense experience (phantasms), and knowledge of which sense experiences lead to certain others (e.g. the approach of fire leads to sensations of warmth). This sort of knowledge, Hobbes wrote, is 'absolute', for it is capable of attaining a level of perfect certainty. As an example of this type of knowledge, Hobbes cites the claims involved in natural and civil histories (EW 3, 71), those that rely on memory (or 'decaying sense' – see previous section). There seems to be no reason why he would not also have held that first-person claims about present sensations count as factual knowledge. For example, 'I am seeing a lion' is presumably an example of factual knowledge.

More importantly, Hobbes claimed that factual knowledge is *not* philosophical knowledge *nor* even uniquely human, for 'although Sense and Memory of things, which are common to man and all living creatures, be knowledge, yet because they are given us immediately by nature, and not gotten by ratiocination, they are not philosophy' (EW 1, 3). So, even animals have factual knowledge; even a zebra can know that it is sensing a lion. Although this kind of knowledge is important for Hobbes in that it provides the starting point for his mechanistic investigations (as we have seen in the previous section), it is the philosopher's knowledge – conditional knowledge – that often involves deeper accounts of the world. Indeed, the distinguishing mark of conditional knowledge, Hobbes wrote above, is that it requires 'reason', or in Hobbes's terminology, 'ratiocination'.

We saw earlier in this chapter that Hobbes defined philosophy as knowledge of causes and effects *via* 'true ratiocination' (EW 1, 3). In the passage above, Hobbes claimed that natural philosophical knowledge – that is, conditional knowledge – requires the use of reason, that is, the use of ratiocination. His understanding of this notion is crucial for our purposes:

> By RATIOCINATION, I mean *computation*. Now to compute, is either to collect the sum of many things that are added together, or to know what remains when one thing is taken out of another. *Ratiocination,* therefore, is the same with *addition* and *subtraction*. (EW 1, 3; cf. EW 3, 29f.)

Hobbes was firm in his conviction that all reasoning is computational, and this meant for him that all reasoning reduces in the end to the addition and subtraction of ideas or words. For example, from the addition of the ideas of body, animated, and rational, one rightly compounds the idea of 'man' (EW 1, 4). Likewise, 'of the several conceptions of *four sides, equality of sides, and right angles,* is compounded the conception of a *square*' (EW 1, 4). And the computation can proceed through subtraction as well: from the idea of a square, one can presumably subtract the idea of 'equality of sides' to arrive at the idea of a rectangle. Both of these are paradigm cases of 'true ratiocination', or proper reasoning.

Two points must be emphasized here. First, when it comes to proper ratiocination, Hobbes placed great importance upon language. In order for science to be successful, we must be able to set up words that stand for things. This in turn facilitates scientific ratiocination *via* computations with words. While there is much that can be said about Hobbes's views on language and its role in reasoning, it suffices for our purposes simply to note this in passing. Second, this view of reasoning (and the method it uses, discussed below) clearly depends upon having correct definitions. In this respect, Hobbes was often seen as employing a 'Euclidean method' when it comes to natural philosophy. Euclid had a dramatic impact on him, for he became enamoured with the geometrical method's ability to produce deductive certainty. Indeed, Hobbes believed geometry was the paradigm example of a demonstrative science, and therefore it should be the model for all other sciences. As such, he developed a method for natural philosophy based on the model of geometrical demonstrations.

3.2.2. The method of analysis and the method of synthesis

In a passage that neatly summarizes the thread of this chapter, Hobbes described his scientific methodology:

> The first beginnings, therefore, of knowledge, are the phantasms of sense and imagination; and that there be such phantasms we know well enough by nature; but to know why they be, or from what causes they proceed, is the work of ratiocination; which consists . . . in *composition*, and *division* or *resolution*. There is therefore no method, by which we find out the causes of things, but is either *compositive* or *resolutive*, or *partly compositive*, and *partly resolutive*. And the resolutive is commonly called *analytical* method, as the compositive is called *synthetical*. (EW 1, 66)

In this passage, Hobbes declared that philosophical knowledge begins with our phantasms, knowledge of which is merely factual. Further knowledge, such as that involved in discovering the *causes* of our phantasms, is philosophical knowledge and thus requires ratiocination. In particular, Hobbes wrote above that ratiocination is to be employed in the methods of *analysis* and *synthesis*. These two ways of reasoning stand at the heart of Hobbes's account of how we gain philosophical knowledge.

Hobbes did not invent the method of analysis and synthesis. While I do not mean to suggest that there is a direct line of influence from previous thinkers to Hobbes, it should be noted that a similar method was expounded by the 'School of Padua', a sixteenth century Italian school of thought. The School of Padua directly influenced Galileo with respect to analysis and synthesis, and it is possible that Galileo influenced Hobbes in this respect. However, Hobbes's particular application of this method is unique to him, and is worthy of attention. Moreover, it is often found to be the most perplexing feature of Hobbes's philosophy.

Here is Hobbes's understanding of analysis and synthesis:

ANALYSIS *is ratiocination from the supposed construction or generation of a thing to the efficient cause or coefficient causes of that which is constructed or generated. And* SYNTHESIS *is ratiocination from the first causes of the construction, continued through all the middle causes till we come to the thing itself which is constructed or generated.* (EW I, 312)

In other words, analysis involves reasoning from the effect to the (possible) causes of that effect. Synthesis involves reasoning from the (possible) causes to the effects of that cause.

Given that Hobbes conceived of philosophy as involving an investigation of causes from knowledge of their effects, and an investigation of effects from knowledge of their causes, it comes as no surprise that Hobbes found causal analysis and synthesis to be the proper methods of philosophy. He did not give us much detail about the application of these methods, but he did offer an example involving light (cf. EW 1, 77ff.). This example makes it clear that Hobbes understood analysis to be preliminary to synthesis.

First, we notice that whenever we perceive light, there is always a 'fountain of light, without which we cannot have any perception of light' (EW 1, 78), and so the occurrence of that source is causally necessary to the occurrence of light. Second, we observe that there must be a transparent medium through which the light can travel, 'and, therefore, the concurrence of transparency is also necessary to the generation of light' (EW 1, 78). Next, 'we observe our own body . . . [and discover] that a fitting disposition of the organs to receive impressions from without is likewise a necessary part of the cause of light' (EW 1, 78). Finally, we notice that since any particular size and shape of the light source is irrelevant to its generation of light, 'it remains, therefore, that the action, by which light is generated, is motion only in the parts of the object', for the absence of motion in the production of light 'cannot be conceived' (EW 1, 78). The transparent medium and sensory organs causally contribute by 'continuing' that motion (EW 1, 78f.).

Having analysed light (the sensory effect) into this sequence of concurrent causes, Hobbes concludes thus:

And in this manner the cause of light may be made up of motion continued from the original of the same motion, to the original of vital motion, light being nothing but the alteration of vital motion, made by the impression upon it of motion continued from the object. . . . In the mean time it is manifest that in the searching out of causes, there is need partly of the analytical, and partly of the synthetical method; of the analytical, to conceive how circumstances conduce severally to the production of effects; and of the synthetical, for the adding together and compounding of what they can effect singly by themselves. (EW 1, 79)

In other words, analysis reveals that the cause of light is motion of imperceptible particles from a certain source, through a medium of transparent imperceptible particles, and the continuation of that motion by the imperceptible particles that make up the eyeball (and at this point, it is now a 'vital' motion). All of these 'conduce severally' to the causal production of the phantasm of light. Note that in this example, Hobbes reasoned from the observable effect (the phantasm of light) to the causal ancestors of that effect. It is precisely this direction of reasoning that makes it *analysis,* and the analysis ended in the 'self-evident' principle of motion, which Hobbes maintained is where all analysis should end (EW 1, 69), as we saw in the last section (Section 3.1.1).

Having performed the analysis, we are then in a position to perform synthesis. Here Hobbes's view is slightly more perplexing, but
his basic position is that once we have the first principles causally
responsible for a given effect, we can then, by way of logical demonstration, derive the effects from definitions of their causes. In
other words, given adequate definitions of mechanical first principles (such as motion, body, shape etc.), we are in a position to
show how light is generated from causes by starting with definitions
of the causes, that is, the first principles, and using them in the
propositions that make up our demonstration. While it may be difficult to see why Hobbes believed this method was proper to natural
science, it is not difficult to see the influence of Euclidean geometry, for the geometer begins with non-controversial definitions
and propositions and derives conclusions from them. Hobbes too
believed that natural philosophy should follow this method. Thus,
he took certain basic mechanical principles, such as the principle
of motion, to be those self-evident principles from which all other
effects could be derived, and they could be derived by way of demonstrations that utilize accurate definitions.

But there is a *crucial* difference between the knowledge generated
by the geometer and the knowledge generated by a similar method
in natural philosophy. Hobbes held that unlike geometry, natural
science can only speculate about the causes of phantasms, and thus
the conclusions arrived at by this method are always tentative and
never certain. In geometry, however, one can achieve deductive certainty from principles having to do with geometric entities (e.g. line,
shape etc.). One cannot achieve this kind of certainty in natural
philosophy for this reason: in geometry we *know* the causes of geometrical objects, but we do not know the causes of natural bodies:

Geometry therefore is demonstrable, for the lines and figures
from which we reason are drawn and described by ourselves;
and civil philosophy is demonstrable, because we make the
commonwealth ourselves. But because of natural bodies we
know not the construction, but seek it from effects, there lies
no demonstration of what the causes be we seek for, but only of
what they may be. (EW 7, 184)

We know the causes of geometrical objects, for *we* are the causes,
as *we* construct lines, shapes and so on. On the other hand, we do

not have knowledge of the causes of natural bodies, or the causes of our phantasms.

Therefore, when it comes to our knowledge of nature's ways, the human situation makes all such knowledge *conditional:* it relies on certain conjectures about the causes of our phantasms (e.g. 'If the cause of X has property Y, then X will also have property Z'). It is for this reason that Hobbes remarked that he was not giving a definitive account of sense perception, but only a 'possible' one (EW 1, 388). Similarly, it should be noted that in the passage previously quoted in which he is discussing light, Hobbes remarked that 'the cause of light *may* be made up of motion continued from the original of the same motion' (EW 1, 79; my emphasis), a sign again of the hypothetical nature of his method.

Finally, given this crucial difference between geometry and natural philosophy, Hobbes maintained that when it comes to the proper definitions employed in demonstrations, causes should be included in the definition:

[T]he reason why I say that the cause and generation of such things, as have any cause of generation, ought to enter into their definitions, is this. The end of science is the demonstration of the causes and generations of things; which if they be not in the definitions, . . . they will not be found in any further conclusion deduced from that; and, therefore, by proceeding in this manner, we shall never come to science; which is against the scope and intention of demonstration. (EW 1, 83)

Ideally, natural philosophy (or 'science') would emulate geometry by including lucid causal definitions, thereby permitting secure deductions. But since this is not the case, the pursuit of knowledge of natural causes must remain conjectural.

In the end, then, Hobbes's epistemological view was that we only achieve complete certainty about those things for which we know the causes, and this limits certainty to those things within the contents of our phantasms. The primary type of knowledge here is what Hobbes called 'factual knowledge', and even animals have this kind of knowledge. Given Hobbes's mechanistic account of sensation discussed earlier in the chapter, it is perhaps true that this conclusion was inevitable. After all, one cannot 'see' beyond one's phantasms in order to obtain certainty about their causes.

And Hobbes was keenly aware of this consequence of his mechanistic theory of sensation (cf. EW 7, 82). Knowledge of the natural world, obtained through analysis and synthesis, must forever remain hypothetical in nature, as it necessarily involves conjecture about the causes of our phantasms. Although Hobbes's method of knowledge acquisition may be well motivated, parts of it will seem alien to the contemporary reader.

3.3. CONCLUSION: HOBBES THE EMPIRICIST

Hobbes's methodology for natural philosophy and the acquisition of knowledge is bound to strike the contemporary reader as fundamentally misguided. It places no emphasis on observation and experimentation, and in this respect was directly opposed to Bacon's inductive method of acquiring knowledge of nature. Indeed, the method places central importance upon deriving conclusions from properly defined mechanical principles. In addition, it places central importance upon the framing of hypotheses that refer to unobservable entities that, by definition, we do not sense, such as the mechanist's imperceptible bits of matter. From this perspective, it might appear to be more of a rationalist conception of knowledge acquisition, for the emphasis is almost entirely on *rational* deductions involving definitions, and this leads to the question: why, then, is Hobbes considered an empiricist?

Despite the rationalist elements in Hobbes's methodology, he counts as an empiricist for at least two reasons. First, he insisted throughout his career that *all* ideas derive from experience. A second and related point is that in order for the Hobbesian method to get underway, the empiricist beginnings must be in place. In other words, one cannot employ the method of acquiring knowledge without first having experienced the appropriate phantasms. Thus, although his method in natural philosophy clearly has rationalist elements, empirical investigation provides the foundational starting point for the entire philosophical system.

Even though Hobbes's methodology was not widely endorsed – indeed, it was widely rejected – his philosophy as a whole proved influential. He delivered detailed mechanistic accounts in a time when mechanism was on the rise, and Scholasticism was in decline. He was also a remarkably keen thinker, whose philosophy exhibits a systematic unity rarely seen in the writings of others. It is also worth noting that his materialism and determinism, though not popular during Hobbes's time, contain insights of perennial importance, and indeed versions of them are widely endorsed today. For these and other reasons, Hobbes's place in the history of philosophy is secure.

CHAPTER 4

PIERRE GASSENDI (1592–1655)

Pierre Gassendi was born in the village of Champtercier in the south of France on 22 January 1592. He was born after Hobbes was born and died before Hobbes died, and his life partially overlapped with those of Bacon and Robert Boyle (Chapter 5). He is the only empiricist in this book from the Continent, yet he exerted significant influence on thinkers from the UK and on the Continent. He met Hobbes during the latter's travels with the Cavendish family in France, and the two became friends and in some ways philosophical allies. His work had an impact on Boyle too, as we shall see in the next chapter. He became famous during his lifetime for his contributions to the new science, and especially for his revival of a type of atomism derived from the ancient Greek philosopher Epicurus (341–270 BC).

Gassendi's early educators recognized that he was a gifted intellect, and while still a teenager he was sent to the college at Aix-en-Provence. He received his doctorate of theology at Avignon in 1614, and was shortly thereafter ordained a priest. He ascended the ranks of the Church, eventually becoming Provost of the Cathedral of Digne, a position that he would maintain for the rest of his life.

Two years after receiving his doctorate, he became the chair of philosophy at Aix. For years, he was required to teach Scholastic Aristotelianism as part of the curriculum, but like all the empiricists discussed in this book, he became increasingly dissatisfied with it. This is clear enough from the title of his first published work in 1624, *Paradoxical Exercises Against the Aristotelians*. During his quest to challenge the widely accepted Aristotelianism, he developed his interest in reviving an ancient school of atomism rooted in the philosophy of Epicurus. Just as Aquinas had attempted to

'Christianize' Aristotle (cf. Chapter 1, Section 1.2.2), Gassendi made it one of his intellectual goals to modify Epicurean atomism to make it amenable to Christianity.

With the help of a number of wealthy patrons and friends, Gassendi was able to publish a number of works, and his interests were vast. He published thoughts on astronomical observations, as well as a tract on Galileo's understanding of motion. He is perhaps most famous in the history of philosophy, however, for his disputes with the French rationalist René Descartes. Indeed, Gassendi is best known as the author of the 'Fifth Set of Objections' against Descartes' *Meditations on First Philosophy.* Hobbes too was an objector, and both Gassendi and Hobbes were in sharp disagreement with many of Descartes' arguments.

In 1645, Gassendi accepted an appointment as Professor of Mathematics at the College Royal in Paris. For the next ten years, he continued to work diligently on his Epicurean project until his death in 1655. The most important result of this project for our purposes is the posthumous publication of the *Syntagma Philosophicum* ('Philosophical Treatise'; hereafter, the *'Syntagma'*). In this work, Gassendi left us a fairly complete picture of his Epicurean atomism. In what follows, we shall take a brief look at some of the key elements of this atomism, and how it fits in the empiricist story.

4.1. THE NATURAL REALM: GASSENDI'S ATOMISM

Gassendi's project of reviving Epicurean atomism in a way that is consistent with Christianity was an undertaking with significant challenges. On the face of it, the philosophy of Epicurus does not seem compatible with religious belief, and in the seventeenth century ancient atomism was often viewed as tainted with atheism. Epicurus was a materialist, who believed even the soul was composed of tiny atoms, a view condemned by the Church. Moreover, Epicurus' atoms were not created, but were eternal and self-existent. Thus, Epicurus did not believe in the existence of a divine designer. From the start, then, Gassendi had his work cut out for him.

4.1.1. The basic principles of Gassendi's atomism

In the *Syntagma,* Gassendi discussed the ancient atomists, and what is good about their atomism and what is to be rejected. After discussing a number of traditional philosophies, including that of Aristotle, Gassendi declared that the atomist view is superior to all its rivals (SWG, 398). He believed that atomism, among other virtues, can explain why 'a thing is solid, or corporeal, how it becomes large or small, rarefied or dense, soft or hard, sharp or blunt, and so forth' (SWG, 399). Whether atomism really has this explanatory power that Gassendi claimed for it is dubious, but we shall see in what follows some of the reasons he believed it did.

But first, the Epicurean atomism must be rid of its 'evil' components:

[W]e declare first that the idea that atoms are eternal and uncreated is to be rejected and also the idea that they are infinite in number and in any [one] sort of shape; once this is done, it can be admitted that atoms are the primary form of matter, which God created finite from the beginning, . . . So stated, such an opinion has no evil in it which has not been corrected. (SWG, 399)

In this passage, we see Gassendi correcting the ancient atomist theory. He declared that atoms are not eternal as the ancients believed, but are created by God at the beginning of the universe. Moreover, there are not infinitely many of them, and they do not all have the same shape. We shall see in the next section one reason why Gassendi insisted that atoms must exist in a variety of shapes if the theory is to be explanatorily fruitful. Gassendi made other adjustments to the theory of atomism, but these are the primary ones that must be made in order to Christianize Epicurus.

Aside from existing in a variety of shapes, what were Gassendi's atoms themselves like? What properties did they have? According to Gassendi, 'atoms have no qualities other than size, shape, and weight, or motion' (SWG, 424). He notes elsewhere, however, that they are also perfectly solid and 'full', that is, there are no holes in them, and accordingly they cannot be divided. Thus, Gassendi did not believe that matter was infinitely divisible. Rather, it consisted of perfectly hard, indivisible atoms.

Notice that Gassendi wrote 'weight *or* motion' was a quality of atoms. Indeed, he understood weight to *be* a form of motion, or better, to be the cause of motion. Since Gassendi was working before the publication of Isaac Newton's achievements in 1687 (cf. Chapter 7), he did not understand weight in the way we do today. He understood it to be that which gives rise to an 'internal tendency' inherent in atoms. It is because of this internal power that atoms are always in motion, and this constant motion is largely responsible for the activity we find in nature. The issue here is about the fundamental source of worldly motion, and it is one that occupied the empiricists right past the publication of Newton's work on the laws of motion. Nearly every empiricist had a view on the issue, and it seems that they all differed significantly. Several things should be noted about Gassendi's views on this topic.

The first thing to note here is that when Gassendi wrote about atoms containing a tendency or 'power' to move themselves, he did not understand this as something that was *essential* to the nature of an atom, as Epicurus held. Rather, God *implanted* in each atom a power or tendency to move, and God *could* have created atoms without that tendency, but he did not. Gassendi emphasized this difference between the ancient atomists and himself:

> The idea that atoms have impetus, or the power to move themselves inherent in their own nature, is to be rejected . . . It may then be admitted that atoms are mobile and active from the power of moving and acting which God instilled in them at their very creation. (SWG, 399)

Another reason it is important to underscore Gassendi's vision here is because it consists of a stance on the issue of where motion comes from: bodies consist of indivisible atoms each of which is created with an inherent tendency to move. Other empiricists disagreed significantly. As we will see in the next chapter, Boyle denied that matter has *in itself* a source of motion. For Boyle, matter is inert and simply transfers motion (cf. Chapter 5, Section 5.1.1).

Second, this God-given inherent tendency of every atom to be in motion is one the most important explanatory principles for Gassendi, as the following passage from the *Syntagma* makes clear:

> It may also be supposed that the individual atoms received from God . . . the capacity requisite to moving, to imparting motion to others, to rolling about, and consequently the capacity to

disentangle themselves, to free themselves, to leap away, to knock against other atoms, to turn them away, to move away from them, and similarly the capacity to take hold of each other, to attach themselves to each other, to join together, to bind each other fast, and the like (SWG, 400f.)

In this graphic passage, we see just how much work the internal 'capacity requisite to moving' was envisioned to do. All natural change was to be explained in terms of mechanical impact between atoms. Even gravity was envisioned by Gassendi to be somehow explainable in these terms, and not by a force of attraction. The fact that each atom was endowed with a tendency to move explains why some stick together, and some aggregates causally impact other aggregates of atoms.

Finally, it is important to note that Gassendi did not seem to understand this capacity in terms of some non-physical entity that lies in the atoms. Rather, however this internal capacity to motion is understood, it must be understood in materialistic terms. Gassendi wrote that in general when it comes to the activity of bodies, 'the fact that the principle of action in bodies must be corporeal can be inferred from the fact that since corporeal actions are physical, they cannot be induced by any principle except a physical and corporeal one' (SWG 412f.). In other words, Gassendi argued here and elsewhere that it is inconceivable how a non-material substance could causally operate on a physical body. Hence, even the intrinsic power of atoms is to be understood solely in materialistic terms. 'Those who made the principle [of action] corporeal', Gassendi wrote, 'and believed that matter is not inert but active seem to have chosen the better course' (SWG, 416).

There is, of course, an exception to this materialistic thesis, and that is that Gassendi believed that we had a human soul that was non-material, yet causally influenced the material body. He also admitted that how this works is not something we can be entirely certain about. Putting this problem aside, we have in Gassendi the only empiricist discussed in this book who embraced a strict and traditional form of atomism, according to which nature consists of indivisible intrinsically active atoms, and everything, in theory, can be explained in these terms: the atoms are 'the origin, and principle, and cause of all the motion that exists in nature' (SWG, 422).

4.1.2. Atomistic sensation

The internal power inherent in atoms is an important explanatory principle for Gassendi. But it is not the only important explanatory principle. Gassendi also sought to show how his mechanistic atomism could explain the appearance of bodily qualities at the macro level, or in 'compound objects':

> [O]ne may well wonder how it happens that if it is true that the only material components of things are atoms and if the atoms have no qualities other than size, shape, and weight or motion, as I have declared above – it may be wondered, I say, how it happens that so many other qualities are produced in things and reside in them, such as color, heat, taste, odor, and innumerable others. (SWG, 424)

In this passage, Gassendi raised the perfectly reasonable question of how it is that bodies come to have certain sensible qualities in virtue of their atomic structure. In other words, how does an aggregate arrangement of atoms make a given object appear to have a certain colour or scent, and how does the mind sense such qualities?

To begin, Gassendi distinguished the three 'inherent' qualities of atoms from other qualities of atoms (SWG, 425). As we have seen, the three inherent qualities are size, shape and weight. Gassendi appears to have maintained that these are 'inherent' in the sense that no matter what changes they undergo, they will maintain the same size, shape and weight. They are, after all, perfectly solid, indivisible and homogenous throughout. On the other hand, other properties of atoms may be called 'extrinsic', since a given atom's possession of one of these properties depends on factors extrinsic to the atom, such as its *position* relative to other atoms.

Having made this distinction, Gassendi gave an account of the sensible qualities *via* a metaphor involving the alphabet. In broad strokes, the account is similar to that of Hobbes (cf. Chapter 3, Section 3.1.2) in that involves tiny bits of matter striking the senses. But Gassendi's employment of the alphabet metaphor may give one a better feel for the sort of thing some early modern mechanists had in mind:

> [A]s letters are the elements of writing, and as from them are produced first syllables, then words, sentences, orations, and books,

so atoms are the elements of things from which first the tiniest concretions, or molecules, are formed, and then larger and larger ones, and miniscule bodies, bigger ones, and finally great big ones. . . . [J]ust as the different shapes of letters, for instance A and O, present different forms when we look at them and different sounds when we pronounce them, so the atoms, depending on whether they are sharp, or rounded, or of some other shape, when they strike the organs of our sight, hearing, smell, or the other senses will create different impressions on them, or appear as different qualities. (SWG, 427)

Gassendi imagined that atoms come together in a variety of ways in something like the way letters come together to form words, sentences and books. Atoms come together to form molecules, then tiny bodies and finally 'great big ones'. More importantly, Gassendi argued in this passage that the *shape* of the atoms that compose a body are directly relevant to the sensory impressions they create when they causally impact the senses. The claim seems to be that just as the shape of a letter is relevant to how it gets pronounced, so too the shape of atoms is relevant to what gets perceived. Some shapes tend to produce an impression of 'yellow' upon striking the senses, for example. Although we get some idea here of what Gassendi had in mind, it may be wondered just how seriously we should take this metaphor, and how exactly shapes can be understood to create sensory impressions.

Gassendi made similar points with respect to the extrinsic property of *position* of the atoms. If we focus on the letter Z, we see that by turning it, we can make it the letter N. Likewise, b and d represent different letters depending on their position. Gassendi concludes that 'the same atom put in a different position will have a different effect on the senses, for example if it is in the shape of a pyramid, sometimes it may penetrate point first, and sometimes land on its base' (SWG, 427). The point is that the position an atom is in when it strikes the senses is relevant to the ensuing sense impression. The same point applies with respect to the *order* of the letters: SUM and MUS have the same letters but represent different words because of the order of those letters (SWG, 427). Finally, Gassendi noted that from a finite set of atoms (letters) one can generate indefinitely many qualities or appearances (words, sentences).

Again, we may wonder just how helpful the alphabet analogy can be: *how* do various shapes and positions create different impressions of yellow and red, for example? Why is the shape and order relevant at all? Gassendi did not answer these questions in any detail, but he seems to have been convinced, as a mechanist, that sensory impressions were the effects of the causal impact of bits of matter, and that since that is the case, the way in which the atoms strike the senses is causally relevant to the sensible impressions they create. In any event, his vision here was influential, as we will see that Boyle employed the alphabet analogy in similar ways (cf. Chapter 5, Section 5.2.1).

4.2. KNOWLEDGE AND EXPERIENCE: THE 'MIDDLE WAY' TO KNOWLEDGE

Recall that Bacon believed that his method of induction could yield at least probabilistic knowledge of the natures of things, such as the nature of heat (cf. Chapter 2, Section 2.2.2). Hobbes believed, as we have seen, that true knowledge involves knowledge of causes (cf. Chapter 3, Section 3.2.2). Gassendi was sceptical about both claims, and developed an epistemological view that took scepticism seriously. But he also believed that we could have a lot of knowledge about the natural world. In this brief section, I discuss first Gassendi's sceptical views, and then turn to his positive claims about the human potential for knowledge.

4.2.1. The sceptics are partly correct

Gassendi was an empiricist because he subscribed to the primary empiricist claim that 'all our knowledge is in the senses or derived from them' (SWG, 87). He did not believe in the existence of innate ideas, and he believed that all ideas are acquired through the senses. So, when it comes to justifying knowledge and acquiring ideas, experience is the ultimate source.

Gassendi was aware that sticking to this strict empiricism meant that there would be certain limits to how far our certainty could extend. For example, his empiricism seems to imply that we cannot know about the essence or nature of bodies in the way that Bacon seems to have thought that we could. That is, we cannot know the inner constitution of any body in such a way that would yield knowledge of why that body has the properties it does. After all, we do not *experience* the inner natures or essences. Gassendi accepted this conclusion. He compared the desire to know the essences of bodies with the absurd to desire to fly like a bird (SWG, 327). In the end, Gassendi's empiricism drove him to the conclusion 'that men do not know the inner nature of things' (SWG, 97).

But Gassendi's scepticism seems to have run even deeper. Recall that Hobbes maintained that in geometry, at least, we could achieve perfect certainty about the nature of geometrical objects (cf. Chapter 3, Section 3.2.2). Hobbes believed this because he thought that knowledge of something required knowledge of its cause, and *we* are the causes of geometrical objects, such as lines and shapes. Gassendi seems to have denied that we can have knowledge even of the essence of geometrical shapes. He wrote:

[T]he mathematician does nothing more than to advise you to look more closely to see what you did not notice at first glance. Hence, the demonstration that he offers you or the means he uses is not the cause of the thing's being as it is . . . but merely makes it obvious to you that the thing is so. . . . Therefore, I conclude that whatever certainty and evidence there is in mathematics is related to appearances, and in no way related to genuine causes or the inner natures of things. (SWG, 107)

In this passage, Gassendi denied what Hobbes asserted: we do not, according to Gassendi, have knowledge of the inner natures of geometrical objects, and we do not have knowledge of the causes of such objects, that is, *pace* Hobbes, *we* are *not* the cause of geometrical objects. Geometrical objects are not things we construct, but are things we observe.

This sceptical side of Gaasendi was partly motivated by his respect for ancient sceptical views, such as those handed down from Sextus Empiricus (AD 160–210). Many of the ancient sceptics gave various arguments involving the limits and fallibility of the senses, and questioned whether objective knowledge on such a basis is even possible. After all, it is the nature of perception to be *relative*: that which appears one shape from a certain distance might appear another shape from another distance. Thus, how can there be any objective knowledge founded in sensory perception?

This challenge is particularly noteworthy in the case of Gassendi. He believed, as we have seen, that the inner nature of bodies was a certain atomic structure, and he wrote confidently about how atoms in motion cause sense impressions. Clearly, inner atomic structures are not perceivable, for they are microscopic. If scepticism about the senses (i.e. the view that we cannot have knowledge of nature founded in sensory perception) is warranted, how could the empiricist mechanist movement even get off the ground? Putting all of this together, we find in Gassendi someone who was devoted to atomism and believed, on the one hand, it was a justified theory of matter, yet on the other denied that we can have any certainty about inner essences of bodies. How could he hold both views?

4.2.2. Knowledge regained?

Although Gassendi conceded much to the sceptics when it came to our knowledge of nature, he also believed that we could obtain a lot of knowledge of nature. The first step to realizing this, Gassendi believed, was to notice that just because we cannot have knowledge of inner natures does not mean that we cannot have knowledge at all. The key is to distinguish between two conceptions of knowledge:

> [A] certain knowledge derived from our experience of the appearances of things should be termed genuine knowledge, for instance when I say that I know that I am now seated rather than standing . . . If you persist in regarding knowledge as the certain and evident cognition of a thing, obtained through an acquaintance with its necessary cause, or by a proof, then on such a view knowledge through experience or appearances would not merit the name of knowledge. (SWG, 86)

If we continue to understand knowledge strictly as that which is 'certain and evident', then even my belief that I am now seated does not count as knowledge. After all, any attempt to prove this cannot rule out *with certainty* that I am mistaken, that my senses are deceiving me, or that I am dreaming. Moreover, Gassendi seems to have believed that beliefs rooted in appearances should be considered genuine knowledge. In other words, in order for me to know *x,* it is not necessary, according to Gassendi, that I have *indubitable certainty* of *x*. As long as I have sufficient grounding in sensory experience, I still have knowledge, even if it is only probable knowledge. And with this conception of knowledge, probable knowledge, Gassendi believed that we could, after all, have some knowledge of the inner essence of bodies.

Since we cannot simply observe the inner essences of bodies, how can we even have probable knowledge of them? Gassendi outlined a strategy for the procurement of such knowledge:

> [T]he truth in question is hidden, lying concealed beneath appearances; we must then inquire, since its nature is not open to us, whether it is still possible to know it through some sign and whether we have a criterion by which we may recognize the sign and judge what the thing truly is. (SWG, 329)

In this passage, Gassendi referred to his theory of 'signs': the view that we can reason from the appearance of certain sensible qualities – 'signs' – to the nature of the atomic structure that causes them. In the *Syntagma,* Gassendi was optimistic that this was the way to obtain knowledge of nature.

One of his favourite examples of how the theory of signs works concerned the existence of pores in skin. Before the invention of the microscope, pores in skin could not be seen. But sweat can be seen and thus is a 'sign' that pores exist. Thus, one can have *knowledge* that skin contains pores (SWG, 332).

Notice that such knowledge is procured by a two-step process (cf. SWG, 333): first, one must *sense* the sign (sweat), and second one must *reason* that there is something hidden that explains the existence of the sign (pores). Depending on how necessary the proposed underlying structure is for explaining the sensible effect, such knowledge will be more or less certain. In the case of sweat and pores, Gassendi seems to have believed that we had at least something close to certainty, for given the appearance of sweat on one's arm, the existence of pores, one might argue, is *necessary*, as there is no other plausible candidate for explaining the sweat. Thus, in this case the relevant knowledge is nearly infallible.

Thus, Gassendi's respect for scepticism led him to develop a theory of knowledge that would go the 'middle way' (SWG, 326): it was not completely sceptical, as it allowed that we can have significant knowledge of nature. But it respected scepticism; it was cautious

and not 'dogmatic' because it acknowledged the limits of empiricism, and conceded that we cannot have certain knowledge of inner
atomic structures. Still, Gassendi seems to have believed that atomism was the best candidate available when it comes to explaining
the sensible signs provided by nature.

4.3. CONCLUSION: GASSENDI THE EMPIRICIST

Gassendi was the only classical empiricist included in this book to
believe in the existence of indivisible, intrinsically active atoms. He
was not the only mechanist, but other mechanist worldviews did
not posit indivisible active atoms. From this perspective, Gassendi
is an important and unique figure in the empiricist movement, for
he represented a genuine alternative in the history of mechanism.

But he is important in the history of mechanism for other reasons
too. He was one of the earliest classical empiricists to recognize
that empiricism, followed to its logical conclusion, leads to at least
a bit of scepticism about the nature of bodies. As we shall see, there
was increasing scepticism of this sort throughout the movement.

Thus, when it came to both worldview and knowledge, Gassendi
was a pioneer on both fronts, and deserves to be counted among
the classical empiricists. Indeed, during his own time, he became
famous for his philosophy and his science. This is particularly evident in the work of Robert Boyle, who was clearly influenced by
Gassendi, and who is the subject of the next chapter.

CHAPTER 5

ROBERT BOYLE (1627–1691)

Robert Boyle was born on 25 January 1627 at Lismore Castle in Ireland. His family was wealthy, and he was the fourteenth of fifteen children. He was born less than a year after the death of Francis Bacon, who had a significant impact on his thinking. He developed a mechanical worldview in many ways similar to that of Gassendi, whom he held in high esteem. Boyle was a contemporary of Isaac Newton and John Locke, both of whom held him in high esteem. He was also a contemporary of Thomas Hobbes, but his relationship with him was quite different, for Boyle engaged in a heated debate with Hobbes about the importance of experimentation in natural philosophy.

Boyle's upbringing was rather typical of someone raised in an aristocratic family. He was educated mostly by private tutors, but also partly at Eton College. During the last few months of his formal education, Boyle travelled extensively, but returned to England in 1644, settling in Dorset. It was here in 1649 that he set up a laboratory in his house, and this proved to be significant, for the experiments he performed there fascinated him, and he became a tireless experimenter for the remainder of his life. Perhaps for more than any other reason, Boyle was one of the great empiricists because of his insistence on experimentation and empirical observation as the road to knowledge. But he was also a relentless campaigner for the mechanical philosophy and its superiority over Aristotelianism.

His passion for 'the experimental philosophy' led him to move to Oxford in 1655 to join a number of like-minded thinkers. Boyle was never a student or faculty member at Oxford, but he did set up a laboratory there, and its former site is still marked by a plaque today. In Oxford, Boyle hired Robert Hooke (1635–1703) to assist him with his experimental work. Hooke would go on to develop a notable career of his own, primarily through his contributions to microscopy. Indeed, he coined the term 'cell' to describe the basic unit of life. But he might be most famous for his dispute with Newton about whether Hooke should receive partial credit for the theory of gravitation.

Boyle and Hooke developed a friendship during those Oxford years, and their alliance is historically significant. It was during this time and with Hooke's assistance that Boyle developed 'Boyle's Gas Law' for which he is famous. The law, which states that the pressure of gas is inversely proportional to volume under a fixed temperature, was published in 1662. In addition Hooke assisted Boyle with numerous experiments involving Boyle's air pump, his most famous piece of experimental equipment, and one that stood centre stage in his debates with Hobbes. The air pump was used for a number of experiments, but was primarily involved in experiments about the 'spring of the air' (i.e. about air's ability to exert pressure and expand), and it was also designed to create a type of vacuum (i.e. a space devoid of air). Boyle's famous air pump sparked debates about the possibility of a natural vacuum, a space entirely devoid of matter (though Boyle himself did not claim explicitly that his pump demonstrated the existence of a vacuum).

Another important development that would come from the alliance of Hooke and Boyle and their connection to other Oxford thinkers had to do with the development of the Royal of Society of London (discussed in Chapter 1, Section 1.2.4). This Oxford group of thinkers is often seen as an early precursor to the Royal Society, and indeed Boyle would refer to 'our invisible college' when discussing the activities of these early Oxford experimenters. It included other notable figures, such as the great English architect Christopher Wren (1632–1723), designer of St Paul's Cathedral (among other things), and the famous mathematician John Wallis (1616–1703), who is credited with contributing to the development of modern calculus. In 1660, the group organized more formally, and in 1663 they received a royal charter from Charles II naming them the *Royal Society of London for the Improvement of Natural Knowledge.* From that point on, the Society flourished and continues to do so to this day. Hooke was named the first 'Curator of Experiments', and Boyle would eventually be elected president, though he turned down the position. The Society was deliberately set up in order to work in the spirit of Bacon, the spirit of experimentation.

It is difficult to exaggerate the significance of the formation of the Royal Society when it comes to the advancement of the new philosophy. The Society provided a formal means, backed by royal authority, for the sharing of ideas and new research. Moreover, they were united in their rejection of Aristotelianism, and this gave the 'anti-Aristotelian' movement considerable impetus. Boyle was one of the driving forces behind the development of the Royal Society.

In this connection, it is perhaps true that no one campaigned more fervently against Aristotelianism, and for the advancement of the new philosophy, than Robert Boyle. His campaign was launched by systematic argumentation designed to show that mechanism (or 'corpuscularianism', as Boyle sometimes called it) was a superior explanatory framework to the Aristotelian one. Boyle did not develop a full-blown epistemological theory, but he remained firm in his conviction that knowledge of the natural world is to be had through scientific experiments and a mechanistic framework for explaining natural events. In this respect he paved the way for other thinkers, such as John Locke (cf. Chapter 6), who sought to provide the theoretical epistemology behind the empirical method of investigation that Boyle favoured. At least for this reason Boyle falls squarely into the empiricist camp.

In 1668, Boyle left Oxford for London where he lived with his sister until his death in 1691. Both he and his sister died within a week of each other, and in his will, Boyle endowed a lecture series – 'The Boyle Lectures' – devoted to the improvement of religious knowledge, and in particular to proving the truths of the Christian religion. There was a long hiatus when no Boyle lectures were given, but now the lecture is given once a year.

Boyle left us an enormous body of work, as he published quite regularly throughout his career. Many of his writings involve detailed reports of his experimental work, but he also left us fairly detailed accounts of his philosophical thinking. We shall begin by looking at the fundamentals of his mechanical philosophy, and then turn to his arguments for the view that the framework of mechanism is one that facilitates knowledge of the natural world.

5.1. THE NATURAL REALM: BOYLE'S MECHANISM ('CORPUSCULARIANISM')

When approaching Boyle's philosophy of nature, it is important to realize that his primary goal was theological, for he saw himself developing a mechanical worldview that would support traditional Christian belief, and in this way his motivations were similar to Gassendi's. Thus, when it came to certain details about his particular brand of mechanism, he occasionally rejected some alternatives on the grounds that they were not consistent with religious belief. Indeed, Boyle did much work in natural theology insofar as he wrote often about how one could tell, from doing science, that an intelligent creator designed the world. But although his religious convictions drove much of his philosophy of nature, it is also true that he remained agnostic about many of the details of his mechanical worldview. This is largely because the empiricist in him did not allow him to draw conclusions about the insensible, and in general he was a very cautious philosopher who drew conclusions only after the most painstaking experimentation.

5.1.1. The basic principles of Boyle's mechanism (or 'corpscularianism')

Fortunately for our purposes, Boyle left a concise summary of the main features of his mechanism, that is, his 'corpuscular philosophy'. It is from *The Origin of Forms and Qualities According to the Corpuscular Philosophy,* a long work published in 1666, and one of Boyle's first systematic expositions of his philosophy of nature. '[I]t will not now be amiss to contract the summary of our hypothesis', Boyle wrote, 'and give you the main points of it . . .'.

1. That the matter of all natural bodies is the same, namely, a substance extended and impenetrable.
2. That all bodies thus agreeing in the same common matter, their distinction is to be taken from those accidents that do diversify it. (*Stewart,* 50)

Here Boyle presented the most fundamental belief of the mechanists, namely, that all bodies are made up of one kind of material substance that is both extended in space and impenetrable. While this may not seem to be a substantial thesis, recall from Chapter 1, Section 1.2.3 that the Scholastics did not hold it. Rather, they believed that there were four *different* kinds of fundamental matter: earth, air, fire and water (the four 'elements'). Thus, Boyle's first point, considered in its historical context, is indeed a substantial one. His second point was that since the matter of all bodies is exactly the same, we need to look for other properties ('accidents') of matter when it comes to the task of distinguishing one body from another. Clearly, they cannot be distinguished on the basis of their matter, since according to his first point, the constitutive matter is exactly the same in all bodies.

The next several points list these other properties of matter, and as was the case for Hobbes (cf. Chapter 3, Section 3.1.1), motion is particularly important for Boyle:

3. That motion, not belonging to the essence of matter . . . and not being originally producible by other accidents as they are from it, may be looked upon as the first and chief *mood* or affection of matter. (*Stewart*, 50)

The point Boyle made here about motion was crucial for his purposes. The motion that matter exhibits is imposed *externally* upon it; it does 'not belong to the essence of matter'. In other words, motion is not a property that 'follows from' or is necessarily linked to the existence of matter, in the way that (say) the property of being extended follows from the existence of matter. Given that matter exists, it follows that something extended exists, since extension, one might argue, belongs to the essence of matter. But motion is not a property of this sort, and Boyle often went out of his way to make this point, as did Gassendi (cf. Chapter 4, Section 4.1.1).

In making this point, Boyle sought to distance himself from the tradition of 'Epicurean atomists', who held that motion was essential to the tiny bits of matter that have it. Recall that Gassendi also tried to eliminate the atheistic elements of Epicureanism (cf. Chapter 4, Section 4.1.1). Boyle sought to distance himself even further from the Epicurean tradition because he believed it was tainted with atheism. Boyle reasoned that if matter is essentially endowed with motion, then God did not originally impose it upon matter. The atomist account was inconsistent with Boyle's picture of creation and divine governance in the world, and we will see some of the details of this picture at the end of this section. But what is more, for Boyle, matter was essentially inert, and did not contain *within* it a source of motion, even a non-essential source of motion of the Gassendian type (cf. Chapter 4, Section 4.1.1).

Finally, in the above passage, Boyle, like Hobbes (cf. Chapter 3, Section 3.1.1), also claimed that motion is the most fundamental of all mechanical properties, for nothing can produce motion except other motion, though motion can produce other 'accidents', or properties (e.g. motion can cause changes in shape and texture). In this sense, motion is the most fundamental property, that is, 'the chief mood or affection of matter'.

Boyle's next point is that motion, as a fundamental property, creates divisions in matter:

4. That motion, variously determined, doth naturally divide the matter it belongs to into actual fragments or parts; and this division obvious experience . . . manifest to have been made into parts exceedingly *minute,* and very often too minute to be singly perceivable by our senses. (*Stewart,* 50f.)

When God adds motion to matter, the motion divides that matter into parts and fragments, thus creating little particles of matter, particles too minute to be sensed by us. As a result, the world is ultimately constructed out of tiny bits of matter, each endowed with the familiar mechanical properties:

5. Whence it must necessarily follow that each of these minute parts or *minima naturalia* (as well as every particular body made up by the coalition of any number of them) must have its determinate *bigness* or *size,* and its own *shape.* And these three, namely *bulk, figure,* and either *motion* or *rest* . . . are the three *primary* and most *catholic moods* or affections of the *insensible* parts of matter. (*Stewart,* 50f.)

In this passage, Boyle emphasized that even the tiniest bits of matter do not differ mechanically from the macroscopic ones of ordinary experience, for they too are hunks of matter endowed with size, shape and motion. By calling them '*minima naturalia*', Boyle meant that these bits are the smallest naturally occurring; it does not follow that they are indivisible atoms for Boyle. It is in virtue of the interactions of mechanical matter at this microscopic level that nature exhibits a macroscopic order.

In his sixth point Boyle drew attention to the fact that other properties of bodies arise from the three primary ones of size, shape,

and motion. When many such particles are brought together, 'there will necessarily follow here below both a certain *position* . . . and a certain *order*' with respect to each other (*Stewart*, 51). And when the particles are arranged with such specific positions and orders, 'there results that by which one comprehensive name we call the *texture* of that body' (*Stewart*, 51). Boyle placed emphasis on the 'second-order' property of texture, as he thought it was an important mechanical property of bodies, one causally responsible in natural interactions.

After noting these other properties (position, order, texture) derivable from the primary ones of size, shape and motion, Boyle concluded his summary list of properties, remarking that these are the intrinsic properties of bodies *considered in themselves,* that is, without considering their relationship to other bodies, and the power they have to operate on such bodies: 'And these are the affections that belong to a body, as it is considered in itself, without relation to *sensitive* beings or to other natural bodies' (*Stewart*, 51). We shall see in the next section what Boyle had to say about the powers of bodies to interact with other bodies.

Finally, as noted above, Boyle's worldview here is a thoroughly religious one and he believed that the mechanical ways of nature vindicated traditional religious belief. According to Boyle, the fact that the world is mechanically ordered as described above is evidence of an intelligent designer. He was fond of comparing mechanical nature to the clock at Strasbourg Cathedral: just as anyone who examines the 'wheels, springs, weights, and other pieces of which the engine consists' will conclude that the celebrated clock was produced 'by the skill of an intelligent and ingenious contriver' (*Stewart*, 174), so Boyle believed it was reasonable to infer that nature – since it is also a big mechanical machine that works by the size, shape and motion of bodies – was designed by a divine mechanical genius. And so, Boyle had a picture of creation and divine providence that was part and parcel of his mechanistic worldview:

> And therefore I think that the wise Author of nature did not only *put matter into motion,* but, when he resolved to make the world, did so regulate and *guide the motions* of the small parts of the universal matter as to reduce the greater systems of them into the order they were to continue in . . . So that, according to my apprehension, it was *at the beginning* necessary that an

intelligent and wise Agent should contrive the universal matter into the world . . . and settle the laws according to which the motions and actions of its parts upon one another should be regulated. . . . And thus in this great *automaton,* the world (as in a watch or clock), the materials it consists of being left to themselves could never at the first convene into so curious an engine: and yet, when the skillful artist has once made and set it a-going, the phenomena it exhibits are to be accounted for by the *number, bigness, proportion, shape, motion, rest, coaptation,* and other mechanical affections. (*Stewart,* 70f.)

More than any other thinker discussed in this book, Boyle linked his mechanistic conception of nature to religious belief. In this passage, Boyle gave us the image of God *adding* motion to matter in order to create a law-like design in nature. At the end of the passage, he argued that the big machine of nature could not have come into its orderly existence in any other way. Yet once God is done adding motion and guiding the parts of the world into law-like behaviour, we are then in a position to do natural philosophy; to 'account' for things in terms of their 'mechanical affections'.

But in addition to explaining things through their efficient mechanical causes, Boyle also believed, because of his views on divine providence, that we could explain them through divine *final causes,* or goals and purposes (cf. Chapter 1, Section 1.2.3). That is, Boyle believed that a study of many of nature's objects revealed that they were *designed* for unique purposes: frogs have transparent eyelids for the purpose of seeing while jumping through areas of dense plants; Boyle observed that fish have appropriate eyes for their environment; moles have feet appropriate for digging and so on. Because his mechanist view was bound up with religious concerns, he maintained that one could explain certain features of the world both mechanically *and* by appeal to the final causes of those things.

The crucial point is that unlike Bacon, who believed we could not read intelligent purposes into the specifics of nature (to do so would be the work of an 'Idol of the Tribe'), and unlike Hobbes, who did not explicitly link his mechanistic conception of nature to religious belief, Boyle's mechanism is intimately bound up with religious belief. Indeed, it is bound up with it to such an extent that some of his views of nature are motivated by religious, as opposed to purely scientific, concerns. He ruled out, as we have seen, the idea that motion could be essential to matter for the reason that such an idea conflicted with his account of providence detailed above. Not only could the world as we know it not have come into existence if matter were left alone, but also, if motion simply followed from the essence of matter, then there is little role for God as the designer of the universe. He also ruled out Descartes' laws of motion as inconsistent with divine providence (cf. *Stewart,* 70). Boyle was a major player in the new mechanistic science, even though his conception of nature was more explicitly grounded in religious concerns than was the case with other classical empiricists.

5.1.2. Sensation and the mind

In the last section, we saw what Boyle took to be the basic properties of bodies considered in themselves. But Boyle believed that bodies possess additional properties when they are considered in relation to other bodies. His favourite way of making this point is again by metaphor:

> We may consider, then, that when Tubal Cain, or whoever else were the smith that invented *locks* and *keys*, had made his first lock . . . that was only a piece of iron contrived into such a shape; and when afterwards he made a key to that lock, that also in itself considered was nothing but a piece of iron of such a determinate figure. But in regard that these two pieces of iron might now be applied to one another after a certain manner, and that there was a congruity betwixt the wards of the lock and those of the key, the lock and the key did each of them now obtain a new capacity. (*Stewart,* 23)

In this passage Boyle illustrated the difference between a body considered in itself, and a body considered in relation to another body. When a body is considered in relation to another, one can see that it might have additional properties – 'capacities' – not noticed when considered in itself. Thus, a key considered in itself is simply a piece of iron with a certain size, shape and texture. But considered in conjunction with a congruous lock, one sees that both the lock and the key now have in addition to a size, shape and texture, the capacity to realize a certain effect, namely, locking and unlocking a door given the appropriate mechanical interaction. This is a property that neither has except with reference to the other.

Right after presenting this metaphor, Boyle used this fairly simple consideration to illustrate his conception of how the mind senses the world around it:

> And proportionably hereunto, I do not see why we may not conceive that, as to those qualities (for instance) which we call sensible, though, by virtue of a certain congruity or incongruity in point of figure, or texture (or other mechanical attributes) to our sensories, the portions of matter they modify are enabled to produce various effects upon whose account we make bodies to be endowed with qualities, yet they are not in the bodies that are endowed with them any real or distinct entities, or differing from the matter itself furnished with such and such a determinate bigness, shape, or other mechanical modifications. (*Stewart*, 24)

The account Boyle gave in this passage was standard for mechanists: sensible qualities are effects of the mechanical interactions of little bits of matter. Just as when the lock and key causally interact, they produce an effect, so too the texture of grass is such that when it causally interacts with my eyes, an effect is produced: I perceive green. Presumably, one would also need to factor in other causally relevant factors, such as the corpuscles of light surrounding both my eyes and the grass. But the crucial point is that sensible qualities are nothing more than the effects of the mechanical interactions of tiny bits of matter.

Boyle did not give many details beyond the lock and key metaphor, and it is far from clear that the metaphor can carry us very far in understanding sense perception. How could it be that when imperceptible particles of matter 'lock' with my eyes, a vision of green is thereby produced? From this perspective, Boyle's account is subject to the same objections as was Hobbes's account was subject (cf. Chapter 3, Section 3.1.2).

In some respects, Hobbes's account is more detailed than Boyle's, for it is clear that for Hobbes, what gets perceived is an idea in the mind (a 'phantasm'). But it is difficult to see what *exactly* the green involved in perception is for Boyle: is it an idea in the mind, or is it to be identified with a mechanical texture? Or is it something else? Moreover, it should be noted that, unlike Hobbes, who was a materialist, Boyle was a *dualist*. That is, he believed that the mind is an immaterial substance, a soul. This raises further complications, as it would seem impossible to give a *mechanical* account of how a substance that bears *no* mechanical properties, a soul, can perceive sensible qualities.

In any event, Boyle did not (clearly, at least) offer this kind of detail. What he did insist upon is that sensible qualities are not, as the Scholastics held (cf. Chapter 1, Section 1.2.3), real existing things, or to use Boyle's words above, 'they are not in the bodies that are endowed with them any real or distinct entities.' Rather, they 'are but the effects or consequents of the above-mentioned *primary affections* of matter, whose operations are diversified according to the nature of the sensories or other bodies they work upon' (*Stewart*, 51f.). We return to this point in the next section.

Despite the lack of detail when it comes to the specifics of mechanical sense perception, Boyle was convinced that the mechanical framework was the most intelligible and best suited for acquiring knowledge. In the next section, we shall see why he believed that.

5.2. KNOWLEDGE AND EXPERIENCE: MECHANISM AND THE CAUTIOUS EXPERIMENTER

In 1674, Boyle published a large theological work, *The Excellency of Theology,* and as an appendix to it, he attached another work, *About the Excellency and Grounds of the Mechanical Hypothesis*. As the title indicates, this latter work was a defence of the mechanist program, or in Boyle's words, 'a succinct mention of some of the chief advantages of the hypothesis we incline to' (*Stewart*, 138). It is one of Boyle's most often cited works, as it raises a number of perennial issues in the philosophy of science, issues having to do with the question of what we should expect from a good scientific theory. In the work, he listed and discussed five virtues of the mechanical philosophy that are not possessed by its competitors.

5.2.1. The excellency of mechanism

After giving a summary of his mechanism, Boyle noted the first advantage of mechanism over its competitors: 'The first thing that I shall mention to this purpose is the *intelligibleness* or *clearness* of Mechanical principles and explications' (*Stewart*, 139).

It is abundantly clear that in offering intelligibility and clarity as virtues of mechanism, Boyle meant to suggest that its competitors, Aristotelian Scholasticism and some others that Boyle noted, are *not* intelligible and clear. Indeed, Boyle remarked that in their use of the notions of 'matter', and 'substantial form' (see Chapter 1, Section 1.2.3), 'the authors have better played the part of *painters* than *philosophers*,' for the theoretical employment of these notions makes the theories themselves 'superficial' (*Stewart*, 140). The meaning and application of such terms is unclear, as they have no grounding in empirical observation.

On the other hand, the 'corpuscular philosophy' suffers no such fault:

But to come now to the *Corpuscular* philosophy, men do so easily understand one another's meaning, when they talk of *local motion, rest, bigness, shape, order, situation,* and *contexture* of material substances. (*Stewart*, 140)

Boyle held that the notions employed by the mechanist are so clear and intelligible that the explanations that include these terms are acceptable even to the Aristotelian. And his reason for this is that mechanism employs notions grounded in empirical observation and ones utilized in common sense talk about ordinary objects. Even when it comes to the imperceptible bits of matter involved in, say, sense perception, the relevant bits of matter bear the same properties (size, shape, rest etc.) as those perceptible objects involved in ordinary perception. Indeed, as we have seen, it is a fundamental tenet of mechanism that the small have the same properties as the large. Boyle's point, then, is that no matter what framework one endorses, one has to admit that mechanism employs clear and intelligible notions.

The second advantage Boyle cites also involves a tacit criticism of Aristotelianism: In the next place, I observe that there cannot be fewer principles than . . . the two grand ones of Mechanical philosophy – *matter* and *motion*. (*Stewart*, 141)

Mechanism makes use of only two principles, matter and motion, through which everything else can be explained. Clearly, Boyle thinks it is a virtue of a good scientific framework that it employs as few fundamental principles as possible. His criticism here of the Aristotelian natural philosophy is that it makes use of too many irreducible explanatory principles. Recall from Chapter 1, Section 1.2.3 that sensory properties were considered real things by the Aristotelian Scholastics, and not merely the effects of particles acting on sensory organs. This meant that there was a real entity corresponding to each sensory quality: roses are red because they have the real quality of redness, and this real quality cannot be reduced to matter and motion, for it is something distinct from both. Boyle takes this Aristotelian approach to entail that there are explanatory entities *everywhere;* it is a *bloated* explanatory framework, and on that score, an inferior one.

The third virtue cited by Boyle may strike the contemporary reader as a bit strange: Nor can we conceive any principles more *primary* than matter and motion. For either both of them were immediately created by God, or . . . if *matter* be eternal, *motion* must either be produced by some immaterial supernatural agent, or it must immediately flow by way of emanation from the nature of the matter it appertains to. (*Stewart,* 141)

In calling them 'primary', Boyle seems to mean that matter and motion are first in production (so to speak). That is, they are the tools that produce everything else in the world, as all the endless diversity in nature is the causal result of the activity of matter and motion. It is not clear in what way this should count as a virtue of mechanism, but it might be connected to his next point concerning the fourth virtue of mechanism.

Here is the fourth virtue of mechanism, according to Boyle:

Neither can there be any physical properties more *simple* than matter and motion, neither of them being resoluble into any things whereof it may be truly, or so much as tolerably, said to be compounded. (*Stewart,* 141)

Here Boyle made the point that matter and motion are 'simple' in the sense that they cannot be reduced to anything else. That is, they are not composed of other things into which they may be broken down or analysed. They are the simple and fundamental principles in which all explanations must end. We might see here a connection with the previous point, and we might wonder whether the points reduce in the end to the same point. The previous point claims that matter and motion are 'primary' in the sense that they precede, or presuppose the existence of natural phenomena. They are the tools from which all natural phenomena are generated. In the passage above, Boyle claimed that they are 'simple' in the sense that they cannot be resolved into other things. But of course, if they could be so resolved, then they would not be primary in the sense of the previous point. Thus, the points are clearly related, and in any event the upshot is that motion and matter are the sole fundamental principles of explanation, principles that in turn require no further explanation.

Finally, the last point that Boyle makes seems to be the one with which he is most concerned. He writes:

> The next thing I shall name to recommend the Corpuscular principles is their great *comprehensiveness*. (*Stewart,* 141)

In calling the mechanical principles 'comprehensive', Boyle meant that, despite there being few of them, they can be used to explain all physical phenomena. That is, whether the subject matter is chemistry or planetary motion, there is reason to believe that mechanical principles can provide the explanations, for in the end, all such subjects, Boyle held, reduce to matter in motion. He made this point a number of times, and often employed an analogy with the alphabet, an analogy clearly reminiscent of Gassendi (cf. Chapter 4, Section 4.1.2):

> [W]hen I consider the almost innumerable diversifications that compositions and decompositions may make of a small number . . . of distinct things, I am apt to look upon those who think the Mechanical principles may serve indeed to give an account of the phenomena of this or that particular part of natural philosophy, . . . but can never be applied to all the things corporeal – I am apt, I say, to look upon those, otherwise learned, men as I would upon him that should affirm that, by putting together the letters of the *alphabet,* one may indeed make up all the words to be found in one book, . . . but that they can by no means suffice to supply words to all the books of a great library. (*Stewart,* 142)

Boyle's point was that from very few basic mechanical qualities, one can generate all kinds of phenomena by way of compounding them in various sizes, shapes and degrees of motion. Recall that Gassendi made a similar point, and thus we have a common thread running through the mechanist way of thinking (cf. Chapter 4, Section 4.1.2). His use of the alphabet is somewhat instructive: even though there are only a small number of letters, one can generate from them countless sentences and books. Boyle saw the richness of the mechanical philosophy in a similar way: it posits a small number of explanatory concepts, which, when compounded in appropriate ways, can be used to explain anything that has a bodily nature. After all, if the phenomenon in question concerns *body,* then it must have the mechanical properties of size, shape and motion.

5.2.2. Experimentation and the status of mechanism

Because of his sustained arguments for the superiority of mechanism over Aristotelianism, Boyle was, in the eyes of many of his contemporaries, the champion of the mechanical philosophy. But as noted earlier, he was, more than anything else, a rigorous Bacon-inspired experimenter. And when explaining the results of his experiments, he never provided mechanistic explanations, but usually just reported the results of his findings. This raises an important question: what exactly is the relationship between his experimentalism and his mechanism?

Although the issue behind this question is somewhat controversial, the answer seems to be that Boyle believed that mechanism was a mere *hypothesis,* and like all hypotheses, it is subject to confirmation and disconfirmation. He did, after all, repeatedly call his mechanism a 'hypothesis', even in the title of his work. Moreover, when touting the virtues of the mechanical hypothesis, he did not place weight on its experimental success, suggesting that it has the status of something not yet fully confirmed. Finally, it should be noted that when he was arguing for it, his focus was primarily comparative: he argued that it is a *better hypothesis* than its competitors, and this again suggests that Boyle believed it was not something about which we could be certain yet.

Bearing this in mind, it then seems fair to say that Boyle believed that nothing trumps experimentation, and even mechanism is subject to disconfirmation. The way to knowledge of nature is primarily through the laboratory for Boyle. But mechanism, as a *theoretical* framework for natural philosophical explanation, Boyle argued, is the best game in town.

5.3. CONCLUSION: BOYLE THE EMPIRICIST

In tracing the history of classical empiricism up through Boyle, one should not fail to notice the development of the movement. Bacon pushed hard for experimentation in natural philosophy, and Boyle was clearly influenced by Bacon. Indeed, it seems no one during the period gained as much fame as Boyle did for avidly pursuing experiments. Gassendi too was an avid experimenter. Hobbes, on the other hand, developed a methodology according to which such experimentation was to some degree pointless when it came to acquiring knowledge of nature.

But Boyle was also a tireless campaigner for mechanism, and in this respect he does bear close ties to Hobbes, who also put forth an explicitly mechanist worldview. Gassendi articulated a version of mechanism according to which nature consisted of indivisible, intrinsically active atoms. Although Boyle refrained from such a strict atomism, his views were otherwise rather similar to those of Gassendi. It is difficult, however, to see that Bacon was quite the mechanist that Gassendi, Boyle and Hobbes were, for although Bacon rejected Aristotelianism, he showed little awareness that mathematical notions might be useful to the study of nature. From this perspective, Boyle had more in common with Hobbes and Gassendi, as the mechanist programme viewed the primary mechanical qualities (size, shape etc.) in quantitative terms.

Boyle integrated two crucial components of the empiricist movement that until now had been largely distinct: mechanism and experimentalism. Although Gassendi too advocated both mechanism and experimentalism, Boyle emphasized both of them more than any other classical empiricist, as he was firm in his conviction that both would yield knowledge. Clearly, he is an empiricist, one who emphasized sensory observation *via* experimentation as a means to knowing the world.

But like Bacon and Hobbes, Boyle did not develop a full-blown theory of knowledge that would underlie or complement this mechanical and experimental movement. That theory would find its fullest development in the hands of John Locke, the subject of the next chapter.

CHAPTER 6

JOHN LOCKE (1632–1704)

John Locke was born on 29 August 1632 in the county of Somerset in southwest England. He lived during the most tumultuous political and intellectual period in English history, and he played a role in many of the events that made it so tumultuous. He made important contributions not only to the empiricist movement, but also to education and political theory. His work was widely recognized, and by the time of his death, he was one of the most famous intellectuals (along with Isaac Newton) in all of Europe.

In 1647 at the age of 15, Locke entered the prestigious Westminster School in London. At the time, Charles I was King of England, but he was soon beheaded just down the road from the school at Whitehall in 1649. Locke and his fellow students were prohibited from witnessing the beheading, an event that marked the beginning of a period during which there was no royal monarchy in England. The event was significant in Locke's life. It marked the beginning of decades of turbulent political times, which influenced Locke's thinking. This is especially the case when the monarchy was restored to Charles II in 1660. (More on this to come.)

After excelling at Westminster, Locke was admitted to Christ Church, Oxford University in 1652. He was there on scholarship and eventually was granted a Senior Studentship, a rank that entitled him to room and board for life at Christ Church. While at Oxford, Locke learned the traditional curriculum involving classical languages and literature, as well as a large dose of Scholastic Aristotelianism. He graduated with a Bachelor of Arts from Oxford in 1656, and quickly took up posts teaching Greek and rhetoric. When he was not teaching, he was developing other interests, including philosophical ones. But he gradually became

most interested in medicine, earning his right to practice as a
medical doctor in 1675.

Perhaps the most significant event of Locke's life occurred in the
summer of 1666, when he met Anthony Ashley Cooper (1621–1683).
Lord Ashley, as he was then called, was impressed with Locke,
and invited him to become his personal secretary and physician.
Locke accepted the offer, and took up residence with Lord Ashley
in London in 1667. The following year, Locke was called upon to
perform a dangerous surgery on Lord Ashley. The operation was a
success, as Ashley made a remarkable recovery. This served to further Locke's standing with Ashley, and the two became close confi-
dants, an alliance that would impact the remainder of Locke's life.

Ashley was a shrewd politician and held a number of important
political posts. In 1672 under Charles II, he became the first Earl
of Shaftesbury and Lord Chancellor of England. The latter position
was the highest legal position one could attain, and one held previously by Francis Bacon. But like Bacon, Shaftesbury (as Ashley was
now called) would not hold the office for long. The King dismissed
Shaftesbury, largely due to the latter's attempts to block the ascension
to the throne of the King's brother, James II, a Roman Catholic who
was in favour of absolute monarchy. Many, including Shaftesbury,
were distrustful of such a King, and plotted to change the line of the
throne. When Shaftesbury was dismissed, Locke was temporarily
out of a job, for upon Shaftesbury's appointment as Lord Chancellor,
Locke had been appointed Secretary to the Council of Trade. Locke
then went back to Oxford to resume his studies, and it was then that
he was awarded a Bachelor of Medicine from Oxford in 1675.

Shortly after this, Locke travelled to France and spent the next
four years there absorbing French intellectual life. During this time,
Shaftesbury's political troubles increased. He spent a year in the
Tower of London, and when Locke returned from France in 1679,
Shaftesbury was again involved in a dangerous political plot. This
time he was involved with a group attempting to have the Duke of
Monmouth, James Scott, the illegitimate son of Charles II and a
Protestant, take over the throne. The extent of Locke's involvement
in this plot is not entirely clear, as he led a somewhat secretive life
in Oxford at this point in time, but many believe that he was probably involved. Eventually, the Duke of Monmouth was arrested,
and this prompted Shaftesbury to flee to Holland in 1682. He died
there less than a year later.

But Locke's long-time affiliation with Shaftesbury put him under suspicion. Matters got worse when, in the summer of 1683, a number of Shaftesbury's sympathizers were arrested for plotting against Charles II and his brother. Locke, who may not have been involved with this plot either, was now under greater suspicion, and so he too fled to Holland in 1683. A year after he fled, his Studentship at Oxford was revoked. Locke did not return until 1689, and he lived in Holland for some time under the name Dr. van der Linden. The English demanded his extradition, but the Dutch refused.

Locke's time in self-imposed exile proved to be useful, for it was then that he completed his most famous works. He returned to England in 1689, after James II was overthrown, and William and Mary were given the crown. This is known as the 'Glorious Revolution', since it was a peaceful one. Shortly after his return, Locke published in 1690 his masterpiece in political theory, *Two Treatises of Civil Government*. In this work, Locke put forth a liberal theory of state that appealed to natural law and natural rights, including natural property rights, and the government's responsibility to protect that property. The work was enormously influential, inspiring Locke's contemporaries, as well as the founding fathers of America, and many others still today.

In that same year after he returned from Holland, Locke published the work we shall focus on in this chapter, *An Essay Concerning Human Understanding* (hereafter, the *Essay*). It is an enormous work – the standard edition is over 700 pages – and is broken into four books: 'Of Innate Notions', 'Of Ideas', 'Of Words', and 'Of Knowledge and Opinion'. Together the four books cover a wide array of philosophical topics: innate ideas, sensible qualities, mechanism, philosophy of language, knowledge, as well as others. It was an instant hit, as Locke became famous in England and elsewhere shortly after its publication.

During the years 1690 and 1704, Locke continued his studies, despite his failing health, and published a few more works, including *Some Thoughts Concerning Education* in 1693, and *The Reasonableness of Christianity* in 1695. He also served as Commissioner of the Board of Trade from 1696–1700, though he turned down a number of other offers of political positions. He died at Oates in Essex in 1704.

Locke is seen as having exercised significant positive influence over the course of philosophy, and his published works undoubtedly have earned him such distinction. Even at the time, Locke was seen as a penetrating intellect by many of his contemporaries. He was elected a Fellow of the Royal Society in 1668. In this connection, he was a friend of Robert Boyle, whose corpuscular worldview influenced Locke's philosophy, and of Isaac Newton, both of whom held him in high regard. The great German rationalist and contemporary of Locke, Gottfried Leibniz, took Locke's *Essay* so seriously that he wrote a line-by-line response to it and titled it *New Essays on Human Understanding,* a title that clearly indicates the work's target.

What distinguishes Locke from Boyle, Newton, and others who preceded him, is that he put forth a full-blooded epistemological *theory* that supported the mechanist movement and the new philosophy of experimentation. In other words, while Bacon, Hobbes, Gassendi and Boyle were all developing a new worldview involving mechanism and an emphasis on experimentation, Locke supported this movement by providing a complete theory of knowledge – an account of what knowledge is, how it originates, and how far it extends – that would be seen as *justifying* the new philosophy. It is true that Gassendi had things to say about the limits of knowledge (cf. Chapter 4, Section 4.2), but his theory is not nearly as systematically complete as that of Locke. If Locke's view about how human beings acquire knowledge turned out to be correct, the new way of doing philosophy would gain additional support. At least, this is how many of Locke's contemporaries saw matters.

6.1. THE NATURAL REALM: LOCKE'S MECHANISM

In the opening chapter of the *Essay,* Locke wrote that his purpose in writing the *Essay* is 'to enquire into the original, certainty, and extent of humane knowledge' (*Essay* I, 1, §2). In other words, Locke's goal was to discuss (i) the origin of knowledge, that is, where it comes from; (ii) the 'certainty' of knowledge, that is, what knowledge *is,* or in what the certainty of knowledge consists; (iii) the extent of knowledge, that is, how far human knowledge extends, or what humans can and cannot know about the world.

This makes it clear that Locke's primary goal in the *Essay* is epistemological, that is, it has to do with knowledge. But it is not until Book IV that Locke finally addresses these epistemological goals. The first two books are devoted to a preliminary, yet lengthy discussion of ideas. Locke's use of the term 'idea' is notoriously vague. He defined it in the opening chapter as 'that term, which, I think serves best to stand for whatsoever is the object of the understanding when a man thinks, I have used it to express whatever is meant by phantasm, notion, species, or whatever it is, which the mind can be employ'd about in thinking' (*Essay* I, 1, §8). By defining it so broadly, Locke lumped together under the label 'idea' many mental entities that some people believe should be categorized distinctly. For example, in using the term 'idea', Locke sometimes had in mind the sense-data that accompany perceptions of external objects: sensations of colours and odours, for example. He also included the feelings associated with internal sensations, such as sensations of pain and pleasure. In other places, Locke uses the term 'idea' to refer to what we usually call 'concepts', mental entities associated with abstract thinking and those things that figure into our understanding of things.

While we might be tempted to fault Locke for using the term 'idea' in such a perplexing way, it seems that he did not think it important for his purposes to distinguish between these types of mental entities. From one perspective, this approach may be appropriate for an empiricist such as Locke, for the empiricists were concerned to show that all of our 'ideas' (concepts, sense-data etc.) derive from experience, and all have a common ancestry. Thus, from the perspective of an empiricist such as Locke, there is a common link between all of our mental resources, and thus a sense in which they can legitimately fall under one label. What is important is that we bear in mind that Locke used the term 'idea' to stand for any mental, or mind-dependent entity, and that he did so explicitly, though somewhat apologetically, seemingly aware that his reader may find this use of the word 'idea' perplexing.

Finally, it is to be noted that although the topic of discussion in the opening books of the *Essay* is ideas, it is through his detailed theory of ideas that we also get a glimpse of Locke's mechanistic worldview. In explaining how the mind gets ideas of the world around it, we come to see what that world looks like through Lockean eyes. Thus, we begin with Locke's theory of ideas in order to get a grasp of his worldview, as we did for the previous empiricists.

6.1.1. Against innatism

In Book I of the *Essay,* Locke launched a sweeping attack on the doctrine of innate ideas. Indeed, it is partly because of his insistence that *all* ideas are acquired from experience that Locke is considered an empiricist. His critical discussion of the doctrine of innate ideas is long, and involves a number of distinctions. For our purposes, we may consider one of Locke's main lines of attack, that is, his objections to what he calls 'the argument from universal consent'. This will give us some idea of why Locke is against the rationalist doctrine of innate ideas before turning to his own positive theory of how the mind acquires ideas.

'It is an established opinion amongst some men', Locke wrote, 'that there are in the understanding certain innate principles . . . which the soul receives in its very first being; and brings into the world with it' (*Essay* I, 2, §1). Locke here referred to the tendency of many rationalists to accept *innatism:* the view that the mind comes to the world already endowed with certain ideas, truths, or 'principles'. If innatism is true, then one main empiricist tenet is false, that is, the tenet that all ideas derive from experience. Typically, seventeenth-century innatists believed that human beings possess innately the idea of God, knowledge of certain logical truths, and perhaps certain moral principles. While it is not clear *exactly* who Locke's target was here, it is clear that many in the seventeenth century endorsed innatism, such as the rationalists René Descartes and Gottfried Leibniz. It is equally clear that Locke disagreed with innatism, and wished to show that it is false.

Locke's initial target is what he calls 'the argument from universal consent':

There is nothing more commonly taken for granted, than that there are certain principles both speculative and practical . . . universally agreed upon by all mankind: which therefore they argue, must needs be the constant impressions, which the souls of men receive in their first beings, and which they bring into the world with them. (*Essay* I, 2, §2)

In this passage, Locke presented the chief innatist argument thus: There are certain true principles that all humans agree are true. Therefore, these principles are innate.

Clearly, the argument as presented by Locke is not compelling, and it is difficult to believe that anyone held this particular version of the argument. Nonetheless, it is worth considering in order to ascertain what Locke believed was wrong with it:

This argument, drawn from universal consent, has this misfortune in it, that if it were true in matter of fact, that there were certain truths, wherein all mankind agreed, it would not prove them innate, if there can be any other way shewn, how men may come to that universal agreement, in the things they do consent in; which I presume may be done.

But, which is worse, this argument of universal consent, which is made use of, to prove innate principles, seems to me a demonstration that there are none such: because there are none to which all mankind give an universal assent. (*Essay* I, 2, §§3–4)

In this passage, Locke launched two objections to the argument from universal consent. First, he pointed out that, assuming there are principles that all humans agree are true, it simply does not follow that they are innate. This is especially the case if one could show that these principles might plausibly come from some other, non-innate source. Second, Locke objects to the central claim in the argument, for according to him, there are no principles that are universally agreed to.

Locke seems correct that innatism cannot be proven true solely on the grounds that there are universally agreed upon principles. Thus, it is up to the innatist to show that such principles could not have come from a non-innate source. But what shall we say about the second objection? Are there principles that are universally agreed to?

The answer to this question might depend on what kind of principle one has in mind. One type of principle that Locke considered, the type we shall focus on here, is *logical* principles. For example, '*Whatsoever is, is;* and *'Tis impossible for the same thing to be, and not to be*' (*Essay* I, 2, §4). In other words, Locke had in mind simple logical laws, such as the law of non-contradiction, according to which a statement cannot be both true and false. Locke's claim, then, is that not everyone agrees about the truth of these principles, for ''tis evident', he wrote, 'that all children, and ideots, have not the least apprehension or thought of them' (*Essay* I, 2, §5). The fact that certain people, such as children, do not even think of them suffices to show, Locke believed, that the argument from universal consent is flawed.

One might object here – and Leibniz did object in his response to Locke – that simply because children do not *enunciate* the law of non-contradiction, it does not follow that they do not know it. Moreover, there is some evidence that children *do* know the law of non-contradiction. They are surprised when they see what appears to be a breach of the law. They do not generally contradict themselves, and they recognize verbal breaches of it as nonsense. Leibniz also suggested that such logical principles are present in the mind unconsciously, perhaps in the form of dispositions: all humans, children included, are *disposed* to assent to the law of non-contradiction, even if they cannot enunciate it. Leibniz famously used the image of a block of marble that contains veins that marked out the shape of Hercules. Such a block is *disposed* upon being chiselled to take the shape of Hercules, and in this sense, Hercules would be innate to it. Likewise, Leibniz argued, humans are *disposed* to assent to the law of non-contradiction and it is innate in them. For Leibniz, even children have knowledge of the law of non-contradiction, and so Locke is wrong.

But Locke seemed to be aware of this kind of response, and he rejected it. He argued that this amounts to saying merely that the mind has the potential, or 'capacity' to acquire knowledge:

To say a notion is imprinted on the mind, and yet at the same time to say, that the mind is ignorant of it, and never yet took notice of it, is to make this impression nothing. No proposition can be said to be in the mind, which it never yet knew, which it was never yet conscious of. For if any one may; then, by the same reason, all propositions that are true, and the mind is capable ever of assenting to, may be said to be in the mind, and to be imprinted: since if any one can be said to be in the mind, which it never yet knew, it must be only because it is capable of knowing it; and so the mind is of all truths it ever shall know. (*Essay* I, 2, §5)

Locke argued in this passage that any claim to the effect that people can know something of which they have never been conscious is incoherent. It can amount only to the claim that they have a *capacity* to know it. But if this is the case, then *all* truths that the mind is capable of knowing are innate, and it is not just logical principles that are innate. Thus, the innatist view is either absurd because it implies that all truths are innate, or it is trivial because it amounts to nothing more than the fact that the mind is capable of assenting to certain truths.

This is the substance of Locke's main attack, though he makes many more points throughout the course of his discussion. It is not clear that his arguments against the innatist succeed, and indeed Leibniz responded with a number of arguments of his own. For Locke, the issue came down to whether we can make any sense of the claim that a person can have knowledge of which she has never been aware. Locke believed that no sense can be made of this claim.

For our purposes, the most important point is that Locke believed the mind came to the world a *tabula rasa,* that is, a blank slate, with no knowledge and no ideas, though it does have the *ability* to acquire ideas and knowledge. We have seen some reasons why he believed this. The next question presents itself: How then does the mind come to be endowed with ideas according to Locke?

6.1.2. Ideas and the *Tabula Rasa*

Having argued that the mind comes to the world as a blank slate with no innate knowledge, Locke turned toward his own theory of how the mind acquires the ideas needed for knowledge:

> Let us then suppose the mind to be, as we say, white paper, void of all characters, without any ideas; How comes it to be furnished? . . . Whence has it all the materials of reason and knowledge? To this, I answer, in one word, from EXPERIENCE: In that, all our knowledge is founded; and from that it ultimately derives it self. (*Essay* II, 1, §2)

Here Locke endorsed the chief empiricist thesis: all knowledge is founded on experience. Broadly speaking, Locke held that there are two kinds of experience that act as 'Fountains of Knowledge'. The first is *sensation,* which we employ when acquiring ideas associated with external objects. 'And thus we come by those ideas, we have of yellow, white, heat, cold, soft, hard, bitter, sweet, and all those which we call sensible qualities' (*Essay* II, 1, §3). The other is *reflection,* which is the 'perception of the operations of our own minds within us' (*Essay* II, 1, §4). Reflection 'furnishes the Understanding with another set of Ideas, . . . and such are, perception, thinking, doubting, believing, reasoning, knowing, willing, and all the different actings of our own minds' (*Essay* II, 1, §4). In other words, sensation provides ideas of qualities of bodies, things external to the mind, while reflection furnishes the mind with ideas of things internal, namely, the operations of the mind itself. All ideas, for Locke, come from one or the other of these two sources, and he believed that there is empirical evidence for this. For example, observation of children shows that 'by degrees' they come to acquire ideas based entirely on their sensory experiences (*Essay* II, 1, §6). This, as we have seen, is something an innatist would dispute.

Just after presenting these basic empiricist points, Locke began to classify our ideas into two kinds: *simple* and *complex*. He characterized simple ideas in a number of ways. He wrote that a simple idea contains 'nothing but one uniform appearance, or conception in the mind, and is not distinguishable into different ideas' (*Essay* II, 2, §1). That is, simple ideas are called 'simple' precisely because they are not composed of other ideas, but are the atomic ideas that serve as building blocks for complex ideas. The mind receives simple ideas passively in that such ideas come to the mind whether the mind wills them into being or not. These ideas form the 'materials of all our knowledge' (*Essay* II, 2, §1).

For example, Locke notes that some simple ideas come from one sense only: from sight only, we receive the idea of colours, and from our sense of smell only we receive sensory ideas of odours. Note that these are *simple:* the idea of 'red' comes to the mind in one uniform appearance, and cannot be broken down into the appearance of more than *one* sensible idea, that is, the idea of red. Other simple ideas come to us by way of more than one sense: our ideas of shapes may come to us from both touch and sight. Again, some simple ideas come to us by way of reflection, such as the simple idea of perception, or thinking. Finally, some may come to us both by reflection and sensation, such as certain feelings of pain and pleasure. The pleasure associated with eating ice cream comes to us by way of sensation (our sense of taste), while the pain of guilt comes to us from reflection.

Complex ideas, on the other hand, are composed of simple ideas, and the mind can be active in its formation of these ideas. Basically, the mind joins together several simple ideas and labels the aggregate of them. There are mainly three ways in which the mind does this, according to Locke (cf. *Essay* II, 12, §1).

First, it combines several simple ideas into 'compounds', and this is the mental operation that gives us ideas of substances. So, by bringing together different simple ideas of sensible qualities we get the idea of 'sheep', or 'man', or 'computer'. In this context, by 'substance' Locke means distinct particular objects, but we shall see in the next section that he sometimes discussed a different sense of the word 'substance'.

Second, the mind also brings together ideas without combining them, and in doing this it gets ideas of relations. For example, by comparing two or more ideas in certain ways, one attains the ideas of 'taller than', 'greater than', and other such relational ideas.

Finally, Locke noted that the mind forms complex ideas by the use of abstraction. The mind abstracts away from its ideas of other things in order to form ideas of 'modes'. In this way, one forms ideas of 'beauty' when considering ideas of certain artworks, and 'a dozen' when considering instances of twelve eggs.

By laying out this theory of ideas, Locke believed that he gave an account of how the mind gets all of its ideas without appealing to innatism. He also believed that he had given an empirically accurate theory, for humans seem to experience the acquisition of ideas in the way he described. Still, this empiricist 'way of ideas' (as it is sometimes called) is not without its critics. But whatever its faults, it did serve the purpose of setting the stage well for the remainder of Locke's inquiry.

6.1.3. Primary and secondary qualities, and our confused idea of substance

One of the most famous discussions contained in the *Essay* is Locke's discussion of the difference between two kinds of simple ideas, ideas of *primary qualities* and ideas of *secondary qualities.* Locke was not the first to make a distinction between primary and secondary qualities, for Descartes and Boyle also made such a distinction, and indeed Locke seems to have been influenced by Boyle in this respect. However, Locke's discussion of the distinction is clearly the most famous, probably because it is the most detailed and articulate. As we shall see in Chapter 8, George Berkeley criticized it at length. Nonetheless, it raises important and perplexing issues about the nature of sense perception, and the nature of sensible qualities.

To begin, Locke drew an important distinction between *ideas* and *qualities*. This is important, Locke noted, because we should not assume that our ideas perfectly resemble the qualities in bodies, and so they must be kept distinct. 'Whatsoever the Mind perceives in it self, or is the immediate object of perception, thought, or understanding, that I call *idea*,' Locke wrote. And when it comes to a quality of a body itself, Locke defined it as 'the power to produce any Idea in our mind' (*Essay* II, 8, §8). Qualities exist in bodies, while ideas exist in the mind.

According to Locke, primary qualities are those that 'are utterly inseparable from the body, in what estate soever it be' (*Essay* II, 8, §9). In other words, primary qualities are those qualities which a body retains under any conditions or changes, and in this sense such qualities are 'utterly inseparable' from the body. Locke cited solidity, extension, shape, and mobility as examples of primary qualities. Again, what distinguishes these qualities as primary is that despite any changes or alterations a body may undergo, these qualities remain present in that body. For example, take an ordinary object and divide it in half. Each half continues to have solidity, extension, and a shape, just as it did before it was divided. Note that Locke is not claiming that each half has the *same* shape after being divided, but only that each half has some *shape*. If it were divided again, it would continue to have these same qualities, and so on through further divisions. This is, for Locke, the defining feature of primary qualities.

Secondary qualities on the other hand are not 'utterly inseparable' from bodies. Locke characterized secondary qualities thus:

> Such qualities, which in truth are nothing in the objects themselves, but powers to produce various sensations in us by their primary qualities, i.e. by the bulk, figure, texture, and motion of their insensible parts, as colours, sounds, tastes, etc. These I call secondary qualities. (*Essay* II, 8, §10).

Locke's main way of characterizing secondary qualities was as *powers*. Secondary qualities, such as colours, sounds, and tastes are nothing more than *powers of* primary qualities to cause in us ideas of the relevant colours, sounds and tastes. A particular arrangement of the primary qualities of a body – that is, the arrangement of its insensible surface particles – might cause one to attribute a redness to that body, or a pleasant aroma. But such qualities are *not* inherent in the object itself in the way that primary qualities are inherent in the object. Although we may speak as though the redness of an apple is an actual feature of the surface of the apple, what is really going on here according to Locke is that the arrangement of the primary qualities on the surface of the apple – the size, shape and texture of its insensible particles, perhaps under certain lighting conditions – cause us to perceive it as red. But the qualitative redness as it appears in perception is not a feature of the apple itself.

But how is it, we may wonder, that bodies produce ideas in us? Locke's answer to this question is somewhat familiar to us by now:

> The next thing to be consider'd, is how bodies produce ideas in us, and that is manifestly by impulse, the only way which we can conceive bodies operate in. . . . And since the extension, figure, number, and motion of bodies of an observable bigness, may be perceived at a distance by the sight, 'tis evident some singly imperceptible bodies must come from them to the eyes, and thereby convey to the brain some motion, which produces these ideas, which we have of them in us. (*Essay* II, 8, §12)

Like all the classical empiricists, Locke rejected Scholastic accounts of sensation, and explained sensation instead in terms of a mechanistic/corpuscularian model. Here we are told that bodies produce ideas in us *via* mechanical impact, or 'impulse'. Like Hobbes, Gassendi and Boyle, Locke conceived of insensible particles impacting on our sensory organs, and thereby transmitting motion through the insensible particles of our organs to our brains. In this way there is no mystery involving action at a distance (cf. Chapter 3, Section 3.1.1 and Chapter 7, Section 7.1.3). So according to Locke, this is the way that ideas are produced in us. It is worth noting that Locke's insistence that the appearance of colour is the causal result of the interaction of certain particles, including particles of light, impinging on our eyes (retinas) is very much in the spirit of current accounts of colour vision.

Does this mean that for Locke there is no such thing as colour? It is sometimes said that Locke espoused such a view, but the matter is controversial. On the one hand, it is true that colours *as they appear qualitatively* – that is, the 'redness' of the apple – are not things which exist on the surfaces of objects for Locke. On the other hand, colours do exist objectively and mind-independently on objects *insofar as they are powers of primary qualities.* This, it seems, is the prevailing interpretation, but whether or not Locke should therefore be seen as endorsing a 'subjectivist' account of colour, according to which colours exist only in the mind, is a vexing issue about which there is much scholarly disagreement.

However such issues get settled, the account is subject to objections we have seen before. But Locke seems more aware of them than previous empiricists. In particular, he seems to concede that it is something of a mystery how the mechanical impact of particles can produce a *mental* entity – a sensory idea that is presumably non-material and so has no mechanical properties – but he noted that he finds it possible that God should have set things up in this way. After all, the motion of a piece of sharp steel cutting against our flesh, Locke noted, produces the idea of pain, though the idea of pain – itself a mental entity – has nothing in common with the mechanical properties involved in the act of steel cutting flesh, a phenomena that clearly involves 'impulse' (cf. *Essay* II, 8, §13). Thus, since we know that steel cutting into flesh produces ideas, and there is no way of conceiving how ideas could be causally produced *without* impact, it is reasonable to believe that mechanical impact is causally responsible for the production of other sensory ideas as well. This, it seems, was Locke's attitude on the matter.

Immediately after arguing that sensation takes place by way of mechanical impact, Locke further argued that 'it is easie to draw this Observation':

> That the ideas of primary qualities of bodies, are resemblances of them, and their patterns do really exist in the bodies themselves; but the ideas, produced in us by these secondary qualities, have no resemblance of them at all. There is nothing like our ideas, existing in the bodies themselves. They are in the bodies, we denominate from them, only a power to produce those sensations in us: and what is sweet, blue, or warm in idea, is but the certain bulk, figure, and motion of the insensible parts in the bodies themselves. (cf. *Essay* II, 8, §15)

In this passage, Locke presented his famous 'resemblance thesis', according to which our ideas of primary qualities actually resemble those qualities in bodies. Our ideas of secondary qualities, however, do not resemble anything in bodies themselves. This is perhaps not surprising given the way that he conceives of the difference between primary and secondary qualities, for if colours are *nothing but* the powers of primary qualities of a body, then their appearance to us does not mirror the way they inhere in bodies, for qualitative redness does not appear to us to be a mere arrangement of primary qualities.

Although the resemblance thesis might seem an innocent deduction from a plausible account of sensory qualities, it came under sustained attack by Berkeley (cf. Chapter 8). Thus, we shall reserve most critical discussion of this view of Locke's for Chapter 8. We shall, however, make some criticisms here of some aspects of Locke's theory of ideas after looking at some of his direct arguments for the theory.

In the process of arguing for the resemblance thesis and the distinction between primary and secondary qualities, Locke gave us a number of arguments that make use of examples. First, when we approach a fire from a distance, the fire feels warm, yet at a nearer proximity one feels pain. Why should we think that the warmth is a property of the fire (as is commonly said, for example, when one utters 'Fire is hot'), yet the pain is not? Clearly, Locke argued, there is no good reason for thinking that one of these qualities is in the fire and the other is not. Rather, a more plausible view is that both the warmth and the pain are in us, and not in the fire. And if this is the case, it is reasonable to believe they are both produced in the same way, namely, by the mechanical impact of insensible 'fire particles' on our bodies.

Second, Locke argued that anyone will agree that a piece of manna (sweet bread) has the mechanical properties of size, shape and mobility, and that it has these qualities regardless of whether the manna is being perceived. Now, manna has the ability to produce sickness and pain in one who eats it, but no one would think that when the manna is not being perceived, the sickness and pain are in the manna. Rather, we are inclined to say that the properties of sickness and pain exist nowhere when the manna is not perceived (tasted). But then, Locke argued, there is also no reason to think that whiteness and sweetness exist in the bread, for just as the pain and sickness result from the manna's interaction with 'the Stomach and Guts', a moment's reflection reveals that the whiteness and sweetness require interaction with the 'Eyes and Palate'. In other words, there is no reason to say that sweetness exists in the bread, but pain does not, for both are effects of mechanical interactions with the bread. Thus, the sweetness and whiteness are also mere powers of primary qualities (*Essay* II, 8, §18).

Finally, Locke argues that his account can explain certain sensory experiences. Consider the fact that a bucket of water might feel warm to one hand, yet cold to the other. Clearly, the water cannot be *both* warm and cold, and is it not plausible to assume that water changes temperature from one hand to the other. Locke argued that his theory 'easily' explains this phenomenon: 'if the sensation of heat and cold, be nothing but the increase or diminution of the motion of the minute parts of our bodies, caused by the corpuscles of any other body, it is easie to be understood, that if that motion be greater in one hand, than in the other . . . [it will] cause the different sensations of heat and cold' (*Essay* II, 8, §21). In other words, Locke argued that the difference in apparent temperature must result from different configurations of primary qualities in each hand. If the motion of the corpuscles in one hand is greater than in the other, then they will interact with the corpuscles in the water in a different way, causing a different sensation. A hand that was recently immersed in a snow bank will experience warmth in the water, while one recently taken out of a hot oven will experience cold due to the motions of the bits of matter in each hand. By appealing to this example, Locke was not only aiming to show that his theory could explain such things, but he was also aiming to argue for the distinction between primary and secondary qualities itself.

As powerful as these arguments and examples may seem for Locke's purposes, they may not establish everything that his theory required. For example, none of these arguments shows that ideas of primary qualities resemble those qualities in the relevant object. And yet it is important, it would seem, that Locke show this, for while it is the causal activity of primary qualities that explains the appearance of secondary qualities, it is the *resemblance* of primary qualities that explains why our ideas of primary qualities appear as they do. Thus, if Locke did not show that the resemblance thesis is true, the door is open to inquire whether our ideas of primary qualities appear as they do for some reason *other* than resemblance, just as our ideas of secondary qualities appear as they do for reasons other than resemblance.

It is important to notice one crucial consequence of the way that Locke set things up. According to Locke, the mind perceives two kinds of ideas, simple and complex. As we have seen, the complex ones are wholly composed of simple ones. This entails that in the final analysis, the mind perceives *nothing other* than simple ideas. In turn, simple ideas, as we have seen, are the causal products of physical *qualities,* powers to produce simple ideas in us. But there would seem to be nothing in this scheme that counts as the perception or experience of the idea of physical matter in general, or as Locke would call it, 'pure substance in general'. Rather, we only perceive ideas of qualities, and we then *suppose* that these qualities inhere in some unperceivable thing we call substance. In Locke's words, '[N]ot imagining how these simple Ideas can subsist by themselves, we accustom our selves, to suppose some substratum, wherein they do subsist, and from which they do result, which therefore we call substance' (*Essay* II, 23, §1).

But the truth, according to Locke, is that we have no idea at all of the matter underlying our ideas of qualities. 'So that if anyone will examine himself concerning his notion of pure Substance in general, he will find he has no other idea of it at all, but only a supposition of he knows not what support of such qualities, which are capable of producing simple Ideas in us' (*Essay* II, 23, §2). This means that matter is somewhat relegated to the status of a *theoretical entity,* for it is a 'supposition' of 'we know not what'. All we perceive are ideas of qualities, for Locke. This puts the concept of *matter in itself* beyond our perceptual grasp. Clearly, this introduces a sceptical element into the picture, and we shall see more such elements in what follows.

6.1.4. Locke on power

The notion of power was important in the early modern period. While mechanism was gaining many followers, strict mechanism was not aligned with any particular view about power, or more specifically, the ability to produce motion. That is, mechanism is the view that all natural change can be explained in terms of the size, shape and motion of matter. But there is the further question about the source or cause of motion *itself.* After all, mechanism (unlike Scholasticism) posited a worldview according to which matter was *inert*, a purely passive substance. So, material bodies cannot move themselves, and they require an external cause in order to be moved. While mechanism as a worldview and as an explanatory framework was becoming more widely endorsed during this revolutionary time, there were differing opinions about the power that brought about the motion of bodies. What is the source of this motion?

Recall that for Hobbes, motion is that explanatory principle into which everything can be resolved. But Hobbes had little to say about the source of this motion, except that he rejected the Scholastic forms as internal tendencies of bodies to produce motion (cf. Chapter 1, Section 1.2.3). Gassendi, on the other hand, believed that motion was the result of the inherent powers of indivisible atoms (cf. Chapter 4, Section 4.1.1). Boyle is equally clear about the source of motion: God imparts motion to matter at creation, and the actual mechanical world with its transfers of motion through impact is the result of God's starting it off (cf. Chapter 5, Section 5.1.1). Locke too had a view about power as a source of change, and his discussion suggests that he was sympathetic to Boyle's view. The point of briefly engaging this topic is to work up to Newton and Hume, for as we shall see in the next chapter, when he introduced the theory of universal gravitation, Newton forced people (himself included) to reconsider mechanism precisely because of its inability to explain power (or force). And Hume presented a compelling scepticism about the very intelligibility of the notion of power (Chapter 9).

According to Locke, we receive the idea of power by observing change within ourselves as well as around us. More specifically, we notice there are regular and constant changes in the natural world, and we deduce that there is something responsible for these regular changes. It is in this way that we arrive at the idea of power, of something in the objects causing change as well as in those things regularly acted upon by such causes. For example, 'the sun has a power to blanch wax, and wax a power to be blanched by the sun' (*Essay* II, 21, §1). In this connection, Locke believed there are two kinds of power, active and passive. The former, he wrote, is the ability to make any change, and the latter is the ability to receive any change (*Essay* II, 21, §2). Thus, in the example involving the sun, the wax has a passive power and the sun has *what appears to be* (see below) an active power.

Locke makes several careful claims about our idea of power. First, he concedes that we never directly observe powers, but only infer them from the changes we do observe. Second, when it comes to power with respect to change, there are only two kinds of change, that is, thinking and motion. Reflection on our own minds is the best source of an idea of active power, for we are able to will the beginning of motion in our bodies, and we are also able to will changes in our thoughts, and these observations give us the idea of active power.

But the most important point for our purposes is that Locke suggests that bodies *do not have* active powers, or at the very least, that we have no grounds for thinking they do. Our experience of bodies reveals that we never observe any idea of the *production* of motion, which is what is required for something to be said to have *active* power. When a body (e.g. a billiard ball) is in motion, it *received* that motion from another body (another billiard ball) and is thus not an *originator* of motion. In Locke's words, 'we observe it only to transfer, but not produce any motion' (*Essay* II, 21, §4). This implies that active powers are found only in souls (and God), for 'the active power of motion is in no substance which cannot begin motion in it self' (*Essay* II, 21, §72).

The conviction that matter is fundamentally inert and contains no active principles was central to the ways of thinking of many empiricists. This may not be surprising. If we are only justified in claims founded in sensory experience and we have no experience of active powers in material objects, then empiricists do not seem to be in a position to claim there are such powers. But as we shall see in the next chapter, Newton would cast doubt on the entire mechanist campaign, and in particular he put into question the claims of Locke and Boyle that matter is fundamentally inert.

6.2. KNOWLEDGE AND EXPERIENCE: LOCKE'S EPISTEMOLOGY

Recall that Locke set out in the *Essay* to address three epistemological questions (cf. *Essay* I, 1, §2):

(i) What is the *certainty* of human knowledge?
(ii) What is the *origin* of human knowledge?
(iii) What is the *extent* of human knowledge?

Locke spent much effort and many pages laying out his theory of ideas before he began to address these epistemological questions in detail. In the first section of Book IV – the final book of the *Essay* in which Locke finally addresses these questions – we begin to see why the detailed theory of ideas came first:

> Since the mind, in all its thoughts and reasonings, hath no other immediate object but its own ideas, which it alone does or can contemplate, it is evident, that our knowledge is only conversant about them. (*Essay* IV, 1, §1)

For Locke, knowledge is not *directly* about anything other than our ideas. As we have seen, experience yields 'ideas' (i.e. sense-data, concepts etc.), and the mind has access *only* to these. It does not *directly* perceive chairs and tables, but only *ideas of* chairs and tables, ideas supplied by way of mechanistic sensory impact from actual, mind-independent tables and chairs. Thus, the mind's knowledge must be directly about its ideas and nothing else. Locke is here simply carrying out the logical implications of his theory of ideas for his theory of knowledge.

Like any systematic attempt to expound an epistemological theory, Locke's theory has its perplexing components. But in broad strokes it is impressively systematic and follows relatively neatly from his empiricist beginnings. This section address the questions in the order they are presented above, beginning with his account of the certainty of knowledge, then his account of the origin of knowledge and ending with his account of the extent of knowledge.

But prior to engaging the three questions above, some further remarks are in order about the connection between Locke's theory of ideas and his theory of knowledge, particularly as they intersect in Locke's endorsement of 'indirect realism' (to be explained in the next section). As we shall see, his theory of ideas may place serious constraints on his theory of knowledge, constraints that may, against Locke's wishes, allow scepticism to enter the picture.

6.2.1. Indirect realism, or
the representational theory of perception

Locke is often seen as an 'indirect realist' or as having put forward a 'representational theory of perception'. For our purposes, these labels are interchangeable, and we shall see why in what follows. While we have already seen some facets of this theory, it will prove useful to review some of them in the context of Locke's epistemology. The theory has four central components:

1. The Causal Component: According to Locke, the primary qualities of bodies *cause* ideas in the human mind. That is, ordinary objects *causally impact* our senses, *via* imperceptible bits of matter, and this in turn causes ideas in our mind. As we noted above (Section 6.1.3), Locke conceded that it is something of a mystery exactly how this occurs. Nonetheless, it is a crucial component of his theory that perception works through efficient causal impact.

2. The Resemblance Component: This is a component we have also seen before (Section 6.1.3). In his discussion of primary and secondary qualities, Locke committed himself to the 'resemblance thesis': our ideas of the primary qualities of bodies *resemble* those qualities in bodies. The ideas of secondary qualities do not resemble anything in the objects, but that is not of crucial importance here. What is important is that Locke was committed to the claim that some of our ideas, the ideas of primary qualities, resemble actual mind-independent features of bodies.

3. The Indirect Component: This component is closely related to the one Locke enunciated in the passage quoted above from the opening section of Book IV of the *Essay:* ideas are the *only* things directly perceived by the human mind. This entails that ordinary objects are perceived *indirectly:* I perceive tables and chairs by perceiving ideas of them. Again, actual tables and chairs cause these ideas in me, as the causal component has it. But the indirect component, though closely related to the causal component, is different from it. This component states that the external world is not directly perceived, but is only indirectly perceived. Perception is mediated by ideas that represent the external world to us.

4. The Realism Component: This component is straightforward enough. It maintains that bodies, or material objects, exist independently of perception. That is, the existence of bodies is in no way dependent on being perceived, and is no way a mere illusion. The external world of material bodies really exists, even if some of its features (e.g. secondary qualities) do not exist in the way that they appear in our sensory ideas. This component is labelled 'realist' because it involves the claim that the external world is *real,* and would exist even if there were no perceivers to sense it. (As we shall see in Chapter 8, one of Berkeley's claims to fame is that he denies the realism component.)

Indirect realism has important implications for Locke's epistemology. First, it brings to the forefront his commitment to the idea that knowledge is primarily concerned with ideas. To know something is to know something about our *ideas,* not about the external world directly. Second, it might appear to invite *scepticism* about the external world. If all we perceive directly are ideas, then how can we even know that the external world exists? Many (though not all) commentators have maintained that this theory places a 'veil' between the mind and the world, a 'veil of ideas'. If the external world of bodies is not at all directly perceivable, if the human situation is such that it is always confined behind a veil of sensory ideas (or sense data), how do we know that there exists anything beyond the veil, let alone that some of those things resemble our ideas? It is possible that the world we live in is one of minds and ideas only, and the sceptic is well positioned to raise this objection against Locke.

As we will see in the following sections, Locke seems aware of this difficulty he has raised for himself. For now though, we should bear in mind that Locke's epistemology is to be framed in the context of indirect realism.

6.2.2. The certainty of knowledge

When Locke inquired into the 'certainty' of knowledge, he was asking in general what knowledge *is.* For Locke, knowledge *required* certainty. A belief that is only very probably true does not count as knowledge, as it lacks certainty. In Locke's words, 'the highest Probability, amounts not to Certainty; without which, there can be no true Knowledge' (*Essay* IV, 3, §14). Locke's inquiry, then, had to do with what certainty consists in, since it is required for knowledge.

The certainty in question has to do with perceiving 'agreement' between our ideas, as revealed in Locke's official definition of knowledge:

Knowledge then seems to me to be nothing but the perception of the connexion and agreement, or disagreement and repugnancy of any of our ideas. In this alone it consists. Where this Perception is, there is knowledge, and where it is not, there, though we may fancy, guess, or believe, yet we always come short of Knowledge. (*Essay* IV, 1, §2)

For Locke, knowledge involved perceiving the *agreement* (or disagreement) between our ideas. It is important to notice that simply *having* ideas is insufficient for knowledge according to Locke, and we shall see this more clearly in the next section. For now we note that knowledge is most directly about perceiving relations of agreement between ideas.

Locke's first example involves a simple item of knowledge: 'the three Angles of a Triangle are equal to two right ones' (*Essay* IV, 1, §2). This counts as an item of knowledge because the idea of 'three angles of a triangle' and the idea of 'equality to two right angles' agree, or are 'inseparable' (*Essay* IV, 1, §2). It is in perceiving this agreement that one attains certainty and knowledge: 'Certainty of knowledge is, to perceive the agreement or disagreement of Ideas, as expressed in any proposition' (*Essay* IV, 6, §3).

In order to clarify further his conception of knowledge, Locke distinguished between four sorts of knowledge. The point of doing this was to illustrate precisely the nature of the agreement/disagreement of ideas that characterizes knowledge. The four sorts are:

1. Identity or Diversity: This sort of knowledge is involved in 'the first Act of the Mind', and is the knowledge that any idea is identical with itself and not with any other. It is the first act of the mind because upon originally perceiving ideas, the mind must 'infallibly' notice that each idea is distinct from another. Such knowledge is expressed by trivial propositions, such as 'red is not white' and 'round is not square'. It seems Locke believed that this sort of knowledge was foundational in the sense that it is required for all other sorts of knowledge (cf. *Essay* IV, 1, §4).

2. Relation: As the label suggests, this knowledge involves 'the perception of the relation between any two Ideas' of any kind whatsoever. This includes mathematical knowledge, as well as knowledge of the truths of morality. For example, any propositions involving comparisons, such as 'greater than' or 'less than' could express relational knowledge. Locke also believed that moral knowledge was of this sort, and he cited as an example, 'Where there is no property, there is no injustice' (*Essay* IV, 3, §18). Here Locke had in mind that the idea of property involves having a right to something, and the idea of injustice involves a violation of that right. Thus, there is a relation between the two ideas. The idea of a lack of property agrees with the idea of a lack of injustice, and knowledge consists of perceiving the agreement between these ideas.

3. Co-existence, or necessary connexion: For our purposes, this is the most important category of knowledge. Locke wrote:

> The third sort of agreement, or disagreement to be found in our ideas, . . . is co-existence, or non-co-existence in the same subject; and this belongs particularly to substances. Thus when we pronounce concerning gold, that it is fixed, our knowledge of this truth amounts to no more but this, that fixedness, or a power to remain in the fire unconsumed, is an idea, that always accompanies, and is join'd with that particular sort of yellowness, weight, fusibility, malleableness, and solubility in aqua regia, which make our complex idea, signified by the word gold.
> (*Essay* IV, 1, §6)

It is important to bear in mind that the idea of a substance is a complex idea composed of an aggregate of simple ideas united in the mind (as discussed above in Section 6.1.2). Knowledge of co-existence involves a perception of the agreement of an idea with an idea of a substance. Specifically, it involves the perception that a certain idea always 'accompanies' the idea of a certain substance. Locke's point above is that in the proposition, 'Gold has fixedness', the idea of fixedness (i.e. the ability to withstand fire) is one that accompanies the idea of gold (a substance). Likewise, the proposition 'water contains oxygen' presumably expresses a truth of co-existence, and so the perception of this agreement between the idea of water and the idea of oxygen is knowledge of a certain co-existence.

This category is the most important one for our purposes since it is this type of knowledge that figures in natural philosophy, and in particular in the new science in which all of our empiricists were involved. Advocates of mechanistic corpuscularianism, such as Boyle and others, endeavoured to discover the qualities that co-exist in bodies. This is surely part of the point of engaging in experimentation and, in Hobbes's case, searching for definitions for purposes of scientific analysis. As we have seen, there was much optimism about the mechanical philosophy's ability to provide intelligible explanations of the behaviour of bodies, and in particular one body's ability to cause changes in another through mechanistic impact. But as we shall see in Section 6.2.4, Locke did not share the optimism of his predecessors, as he saw a number of obstacles to securing the sort of mechanistic knowledge that was hoped for.

4. Real Existence: 'The fourth and last sort is, that of actual real existence agreeing to any idea' (*Essay* IV, 1, §7). This type of knowledge is the one that many believe Locke is not entitled to, as it seems on the face of it inconsistent with his definition of knowledge as involving agreement *between ideas.* It involves knowledge of so-called existential propositions – that is, those that express the claim that a certain entity exists. In most instances knowledge of real existence is knowledge of things that exist beyond the veil of ideas; it is knowledge closely connected to component four of indirect realism (discussed in the previous section). We might wonder, given that all we have access to are ideas according to Locke, whether such knowledge is possible at all, for it would seem to require *direct* perceptual acquaintance with actual objects, and not merely *the ideas of* those objects. But Locke made it clear that knowledge is of ideas, and not objects directly. We will return to this concern in Section 6.2.4.

Locke took this four-fold division to be exhaustive of human knowledge. Having presented what he took knowledge to consist of, as well as the four kinds of knowledge, Locke saw his next task to be one of addressing where this knowledge comes from, and just how far such knowledge of each type can extend.

6.2.3. The origin of knowledge

Experience, Locke told us, provides the 'materials' for human knowledge (cf. *Essay* II, 1, §2, and Section 6.1.2 above), but it *alone* does not supply knowledge. That is, merely having an idea does not constitute knowledge. Assuming that knowledge involves perceiving that a proposition is *true* (false) – or in Lockean terms, perceiving that the ideas involved in the proposition agree (disagree) with one another – more is required than simply having the ideas provided by experience. Locke put the point thus: 'for truth or falsehood, lying always in some affirmation, or negation, mental or verbal, our ideas are not capable any of them of being false, till the mind passes some judgment on them; that is, affirms or denies something of them' (*Essay* II, 32, §3).

But even judgement is not enough, for as we have seen the mind must *perceive* that the relevant purported agreement *actually* holds. Mere judgement is consistent with a lack of knowledge, as one can judge wrongly. The certainty required for knowledge, on the other hand, is inconsistent with judging falsely. Thus, although it is not wrong to say that for Locke all knowledge comes from experience, experience *alone*, understood simply as the attaining of ideas, is not in itself sufficient for knowledge, for the mind must also judge *with certainty* – that is, the mind must perceive the actual agreement – in order to have knowledge.

This means that Locke has set a very high standard for knowledge, for one must perceive with certainty that the relevant judgement of agreement holds. How does the mind come to achieve such certainty? In other words, in addition to having ideas, what according to Locke, is the origin of knowledge involving those ideas? This is the question Locke set for himself at this point.

Although the materials for every kind of knowledge are ideas, and are all derived from the same origin, that is, experience, not all certainty or knowledge comes to the mind from the same origin. Locke distinguished three 'degrees of knowledge' each with its own 'ways of evidence and certainty' (*Essay* IV, 2, §14). That is, each comes from a different source, and consequently yields a different degree of certainty.

First, there is what Locke called *intuitive knowledge,* in which case 'the mind perceives the agreement or disagreement of two ideas immediately by themselves, without the intervention of any other' (*Essay* IV, 2, §1). As an example, Locke cited the proposition that 'white is not black', and 'a circle is not a triangle' (*Essay* IV, 2, §1). In these instances, the mind perceives 'at first sight' the truth of the proposition and the agreement between the relevant ideas. Thus, knowledge by way of intuition is 'immediate' since it does not require that a mind engage in discursive reasoning in order to arrive at it. Intuitive knowledge is the most certain knowledge available, as the perception of the connection between the relevant ideas is utterly clear.

Second, there is what Locke called *demonstrative knowledge,* in which case the mind is led 'by the intervention of other ideas (one or more, as it happens) to discover the agreement or disagreement, which it searches; and this is that which we call reasoning' (*Essay* IV, 2, §2). By employing reasoning, demonstrative knowledge, unlike intuitive knowledge, arrives at the perception of agreement of ideas by way of proofs, or 'demonstrations'. Locke's example of such knowledge involved the sum of the angles of a triangle. Not knowing at first that the sum is equal to two right angles, the mind arrives at such knowledge by demonstration, which according to Locke involves a chain of ideas, that is, reasoning. Indeed, standard mathematical proofs fall into this category. Each step in the demonstration must have intuitive certainty if the conclusion is to be known with certainty. That is, each step involved in the reasoning must involve the perception of an agreement of ideas, and that perception must be utterly clear, and lead to the next step in the demonstration. Demonstrative knowledge, because it employs 'intervening steps', is not immediate in the way that intuitive knowledge is. Moreover, although it yields certainty, it is not as certain as intuitive knowledge, since it requires memory from one step to the next. It is thus liable to error, for the longer the demonstration, the more there is to remember while reasoning, and 'there the danger of the Mistake is the greater' (*Essay* IV, 17, §15).

Finally, Locke claimed that 'whatever comes short of [intuition and demonstration] with what assurance soever embraced, is but faith, or opinion, but not knowledge' (*Essay* IV, 2, §14). Nonetheless, he went on to allow a third source of knowledge that some commentators have looked upon with suspicion:

There is, indeed, another perception of the mind, employ'd about the particular existence of finite beings without us; which going beyond bare probability, and yet not reaching perfectly to either of the foregoing degrees of certainty, passes under the name of knowledge. . . . so that, I think, we may add to the two former sorts of knowledge, this also, of the existence of particular external objects, by that perception and consciousness we have of the actual entrance of ideas from them, and allow these three degrees of knowledge, viz., intuitive, demonstrative, and sensitive: in each of which, there are different degrees and ways of evidence and certainty. (*Essay* IV, 2, §14)

In this passage, Locke introduced the third degree of knowledge, *sensitive knowledge*. This is the knowledge we get from the sensations that lead us to believe that external bodies exist. It is, as Locke noted, the least certain of the three types of knowledge, as existential truths cannot be delivered by way of intuition or demon-stration. For example, the proposition, 'There is a chair in front of me', is an example of sensitive knowledge, assuming I am presently receiving an idea of a chair.

Clearly, one can question whether sensitive knowledge should count as knowledge for Locke. After all, it is certainly possible to have ideas of things that do not exist, though they may *seem* to exist. As René Descartes pointed out prior to Locke, anyone who has had a dream that seemed real can infer that one's present sen-sory ideas may likewise not correspond to any external reality. And there would seem to be no ways of being *certain* that my present sensory ideas do correspond to an external world. And *certainty,* it must be remembered, is *required* for knowledge, according to Locke. Nonetheless, Locke was unmoved by such sceptical consid-erations (cf. *Essay* IV, 2, §14).

Locke responded to the 'dream' hypothesis with two points. The first point was that if we are dreaming, it does not matter what rea-soning we use in these matters, since we are dreaming that we have knowledge of these matters when in fact we do not (cf. *Essay* IV, 11, §8). It is hardly clear that this is a successful response, or even to the point, for even if we are dreaming, there is still truth and know-ledge about the dream world. In any event, the second response is more straightforward: Locke simply denied that a dream could prod-uce the sensations that occur when we are (seemingly) awake. The pain induced by fire is much worse in actuality than it is in the dream.

Even if Locke's second response is correct, there may still be a related difficulty internal to his own theory of knowledge. For Locke, as we have seen, all knowledge is the perception of the agreement between *ideas.* But sensitive knowledge, the knowledge that external bodies exist, seems to require the perception of the agreement between, say, my idea of a chair *and the chair itself.* But this latter entity is not an idea, and perception of *it* would extend beyond my ideas. So, if Locke is committed to the claim that all knowledge only involves ideas, perhaps sensitive knowledge cannot be had. And if it can be had, then Locke's definition of knowledge, according to which it extends no further than our ideas, is wrong. Either way, Locke is charged with inconsistency.

It is possible that Locke intended sensitive knowledge to involve the perception of the agreement between, say, my idea of a chair and my idea of *actual external existence* (or some such idea). If so, this would be in accord with his definition of knowledge. But it may leave untouched the general sceptical concern about whether we can ever achieve certainty about the connection between these two ideas.

In short, Locke maintained that there are three origins of knowledge, each with their varying degrees of certainty. Intuition provides the most certainty. Demonstration provides certainty, though less so than intuition. And sensation provides the least amount of certainty, though it still counted as knowledge for Locke.

6.2.4. The extent of knowledge

We have one more question to address before completing our discussion of Locke's epistemology. The question is an important one for Locke, and having set out the theory of ideas and the nature of human knowledge, he is now in a position to address it: What is the *extent* of human knowledge? In other words, what can humans know, and what are they incapable of knowing given their limited cognitive faculties?

This was an important question particularly in the early modern period. The seventeenth century was a time of great intellectual optimism, as our empiricist thinkers and others were making great advances in science while they overturned traditional Aristotelianism. They believed themselves to be gaining more and more knowledge of the world through experimentation and the framework of mechanism. Locke's question in this context is: What are the limits of what we can know?

To begin, there are two preliminary points to bear in mind about Locke on the extent of human knowledge. These preliminaries follow from the work Locke had done up to this point. Locke's first point should be clear by now, and it is the obvious point that 'we can have knowledge no farther than we have ideas' (*Essay* IV, 3, §1). A person cannot have knowledge of things that extend beyond that person's range of ideas.

Second, knowledge is narrower than the range of ideas: 'we can have no knowledge farther, than we can have Perception of that Agreement, or Disagreement' (*Essay* IV, 3, §2). Locke's point here is that since knowledge requires perception of the *agreement* or *disagreement* between ideas, then our knowledge extends only as far as we see such connections. Thus, the range of knowledge is narrower than the range of mere ideas.

With these preliminaries out of the way, we may consider more specifically what Locke took to be the extent of knowledge by considering each type of knowledge discussed above (in Section 6.2.1).

1. The Extent of Our Knowledge of Identity or Diversity: Our knowledge in this category extends as far as our range of ideas, according to Locke (cf. *Essay* IV, 3, §8). Recall that Locke included in this category any knowledge expressed by the proposition that a given idea is identical with itself, and distinct from any other idea (e.g. 'red is not white'). Thus, with respect to each of our ideas, we have intuitive knowledge that it is identical with itself and distinct from any other idea, and this marks the extent of knowledge in this category.

2. The Extent of Our Knowledge of Relations: Recall that this type of knowledge involves the relations between any two ideas. Thus, 'five is greater than three' is an example of relational knowledge. Locke also included, as we have seen, moral knowledge in this category. Thus, while he does not commit himself to the exact extent of this type of knowledge, Locke believed that this might be the largest category of knowledge since there are always additional relations to be discovered between ideas, especially in morality and mathematics (cf. *Essay* IV, 3, 18). So, our knowledge in this category extends indefinitely far.

3. The Extent of Our Knowledge of Co-Existence: It is with respect to this category that Locke's pessimism was at its greatest. He believed our potential for knowledge in this category is very limited: when it comes to knowledge of co-existence, 'our knowledge is very short, though in this consists the greatest and most material part of our knowledge concerning substances' (*Essay* IV, 3, §9). This is important, for as noted in this passage and above, this type of knowledge is that which natural philosophy and mechanism in particular are engaged in securing. If Locke was correct, the optimism about the potential for a thoroughgoing mechanistic knowledge of the world is somewhat misplaced. Here is why.

If mechanism, as an explanatory framework, is understood as holding out hope for a *demonstrative* science of nature, then it would seem that if we knew the mechanical properties of the insensible bits of matter that make up a body and cause change, then we would be able to *demonstrate* that that particular body will necessarily cause specific types of changes in other bodies.

In Locke's words: 'I doubt not but if we could discover the figure, size, texture, and motion of the minute constituent parts of any two bodies, we should know *without trial* several operations one upon another, as we do now the properties of a square, or a triangle' (*Essay* IV, 3, §25; my emphasis). Just as we can demonstrate the connections and properties between geometrical shapes – *not* by 'trial', that is, *not* by experiment – but by simply reflecting on the ideas of those shapes, so too if we knew the mechanical properties of bodies in this kind of detail, we could *demonstrate* their properties *simply by reflecting on the ideas of those properties.* We would then have demonstrative knowledge of how and why those bodies cause the particular changes they do. 'Did we know the mechanical affections of the particles of Rhubarb, . . . we should be able to tell before hand, that Rhubarb will purge' (*Essay* IV, 3, §25). Indeed, mechanism, because it appealed to *mathematical* properties (size, shape etc.), did hold out the hope for such demonstrations, the sort of demonstrations available in mathematics.

But according to Locke, this hope is misplaced. To begin, Locke noted that our ideas simply do not reveal any 'visible necessary connexion, or inconsistency with any other simple Ideas' (*Essay* IV, 3, §10). Thus, we cannot, simply by reflecting on our ideas, see any connections they bear with any other bodies. This is an obstacle to the relevant kind of demonstrative knowledge. But it is not the biggest obstacle.

The biggest obstacle, Locke argued is that we cannot even *conceive* of what such a connection might be like:

[T]here is yet another and more incurable part of ignorance, which sets us more remote from a certain knowledge of the co-existence, or inco-existence (if I may so say) of different ideas in the same subject; and that is, that there is no discoverable connection between any secondary quality, and those primary qualities that it depends on. (*Essay* IV, 3, §12)

The point here was not simply that we have no visible ideas of the minute textures responsible for the production of our ideas of secondary qualities. Rather, the point is that there is no *conceivable* connection between primary and secondary qualities. Why should imperceptible bits of matter of certain sizes and shapes produce the idea of, say, red, as opposed to the idea of blue? What is the connection between mechanical qualities and ideas? While we can clearly conceive of the connection between the sum of the interior angles of a triangle, and two right angles, such a 'necessary connection' seems to be inconceivable in the case involving primary and secondary qualities, for you cannot *deduce* the one from the other.

It is important to bear in mind that for Locke, knowledge requires certainty, and so if the new science is to yield *knowledge*, it must be capable of yielding *certainty*. As we have seen, there are three routes to such certainty: intuition, demonstration and sensation. Clearly, the connections between primary and secondary qualities are not something to be grasped by intuition, that is, by immediate perception. It is not obvious, immediately or otherwise, why certain primary qualities should produce ideas of certain secondary qualities. And as just noted, sensation – present perception of ideas – also does not reveal any 'visible' connections between ideas of such qualities. Thus, this leaves demonstration. But demonstration requires that each step in the proof be connected to the preceding step in a way that is accessible to intuition, just as in traditional mathematical proofs. But there is no conceivable connection between ideas of primary qualities and ideas of secondary qualities. Hence, there can be no demonstrations involving such connections either, and so there can be no certainty and no knowledge of such co-existences for Locke either.

Sometimes, Locke drew the further point that we will never be able to frame *rules*, or laws, involving the qualities of bodies:

> That the size, figure, and motion of one body should cause a change in the size, figure, and motion of another body, is not beyond our conception; . . . these seem to us to have some connexion one with another. . . . but our minds not being able to discover any connexion betwixt these primary qualities of bodies, and the sensations that are produced in us by them, we can never be able to establish certain and undoubted rules, of the consequence or co-existence of any secondary qualities, though we could discover the size, figure, or motion of those invisible parts, which immediately produce them. (*Essay* IV, 3, §13)

Locke's point here was that although we can conceive *in general* that one body should cause changes in another through its mechanical qualities, we cannot conceive of any *possible* way that ideas of secondary qualities could be deduced, *via* conceptual connections, from ideas of primary qualities. As a result, we could never frame universal 'rules' or laws expressing which primary qualities produce which secondary qualities. But the aim of science *just is* to secure such knowledge in the form of rules or laws.

Having noted our ignorance with respect to knowledge of co-existence, Locke went on to explore the causes of it. He noted that most of the bodies in the universe are too remote for observation, and with respect to those that are not too remote, they have parts that are too minute, such as the internal insensible corpuscles that produce change (*Essay* IV, 3, §§24–25). And so, Locke drew the following conclusion about the scientific movement in his day:

> And therefore I am apt to doubt that, how far soever, humane industry may advance useful and experimental philosophy in physical things, scientifical will still be out of our reach: . . . we are not capable of scientifical knowledge; nor shall ever be able to discover general, instructive, unquestionable truths concerning them. (*Essay* IV, 3, §26)

The point was that the experimental philosophies of Bacon and Boyle may produce many practical benefits, but genuine scientific knowledge, understood as consisting of certainty, is beyond the reach of the human mind.

4. The Extent of Our Knowledge of Real Existence: Finally, Locke's views on the extent of our knowledge of real existence are straightforward. He believed that we have knowledge of our own existence through intuition, and that we have knowledge of the existence of God through demonstration (though we shall not discuss his attempted proof here). As discussed above, Locke believed that we have knowledge of the existence of external objects by way of sensitive knowledge. Again, whether sensitive knowledge should count as knowledge, and whether it is consistent with his definition of knowledge, are issues open to debate (cf. Section 6.2.3).

6.3. CONCLUSION: LOCKE THE EMPIRICIST

It is sometimes claimed that Locke was the first classical empiricist. This claim suggests that that he alone was the first to argue against

Aristotelianism on empiricist grounds. I think this is clearly wrong, for as we have seen, Bacon, Hobbes, Gassendi and Boyle were presenting empiricist views before Locke's *Essay* was published.

Nonetheless, he was the first to do a number of things for the empiricist movement. Locke provided the epistemological underpinnings for the new science and empiricism in general. In previous chapters, we saw that both mechanism and experimentation were (in most cases) important components of the empiricist way of thinking. Locke's *Essay* sought to justify mechanism and experimentation. With respect to the former, his detailed discussion of primary and secondary qualities gave impetus to the claim that corpuscular qualities were worth exploring. With respect to the new philosophy of experimentation, Locke aimed to show how learning and the acquisition of knowledge stem from sensory observation alone, an epistemological claim very much in harmony with the new science being put forward by Locke's countrymen. In general, Locke was the first to give a full-blown empiricist theory of knowledge that would serve as the justificatory backdrop for the movement.

This is not to say that Locke did not introduce some perplexing philosophical problems. For example, a number of elements of Locke's epistemology seem to lead to scepticism. As we have seen, he readily maintained that we have access only to mental contents (ideas) and never to objects themselves. Moreover, some of these ideas do not resemble objects, and we have no clue when it comes to the causal connections between objects and our sensory contents, that is, the connection between primary qualities and our ideas of secondary qualities. Our knowledge concerning the existence of the external world is confined to 'sensitive knowledge', which Locke admits is less certain than other kinds of knowledge. And even sensitive knowledge cannot be had of matter itself, or 'pure substance in general'. Locke was not a sceptic, for he believed in the external world of bodies and he believed, as we have seen, that we can acquire quite a bit of knowledge. But his epistemology and his theory of ideas combine to provide the sceptic with much to be sceptical about: given all of the above, the sceptic could surely argue that many of Locke's claims about the external world are unjustified. After all, if we follow Locke, there appears to be a 'veil' between minds and the world, a veil that prohibits certainty about that world. As we shall see in Chapter 8, Berkeley sought to get rid of these sceptical consequences.

CHAPTER 7

ISAAC NEWTON (1642–1727)

Isaac Newton was born on Christmas Day 1642 in Lincolnshire, England in the small town of Woolsthorpe. He was born the same year that Galileo died, and ten years after Locke was born. He is justly regarded one of the greatest scientists to have ever lived. He made enormous contributions to the history of intellectual thought: he invented the calculus, made important discoveries in optics, gave us the laws of motion, and of course, the theory of universal gravitation. He was also a complex figure with intense interests in alchemy and theology, as well as in the subjects for which he is now famous. He was also a very controversial figure who made a number of enemies throughout the course of his career. Nonetheless, by the time of his death, he was held in high esteem for his accomplishments, and was probably the most famous intellect in the world.

Newton's father died a few months before Newton was born, and Newton's mother remarried when he was three years old. When his mother remarried, she left Newton with his maternal grandmother, who raised him until his mother returned in 1653, but Newton was sent to boarding school in Grantham only two years later. After Newton completed a failed attempt to manage the family estate, his mother was convinced to send him to Cambridge University. So, in 1661, he entered Trinity College, Cambridge.

The curriculum at Cambridge consisted almost entirely of traditional Aristotelianism. However, Newton began teaching himself things that were not part of the curriculum, and he became increasingly interested in the new philosophy. He immersed himself in the new mathematical developments of the time, and in particular, in the works of the leading rationalist at the time, René Descartes.

Before graduating with a B. A. from Trinity in 1665, he was already developing interests in the nature of light and colour, and gravity.

From 1665 to 1667, Newton spent most of his time at home in Woolsthorpe since the plague had descended on Cambridge and forced him to evacuate. This period of time in Newton's life is often referred to as the *anni mirabilis* – the 'miraculous years'. It was during this time of isolation at home that he developed the foundations for much of the work that would make him famous. He made a number of experimental breakthroughs in optics, developed the theory of uniform circular motion, recognized the importance of the inverse square law for planetary motion, and invented the fluxional calculus.

Newton was made a Fellow at Trinity in 1667, and was awarded the M. A. in 1668. The following year he was appointed Lucasian Professor of Mathematics, and shortly thereafter resumed his work in optics. He went public with this work by presenting his 'New Theory About Light and Colours' to the Royal Society of London in 1672, the same year that he was elected a Fellow of the Royal Society on the basis of a reflecting telescope he had invented. His work on light and colours was published in the *Philosophical Transactions of the Royal Society,* and was subsequently challenged by a number of people, but most notably by Robert Hooke, who was the Curator of Experiments for the Royal Society. (For more on Hooke, see the opening section of Chapter 5.) This led to a heated exchange with Hooke. Because of this dispute Newton became disenchanted with the idea of publicizing his work, and he spent the next several years largely withdrawn in isolation. During this time, he pursued alchemy and biblical chronology with as much energy and interest as anything else he studied.

In 1679, Hooke and Newton agreed to put their differences aside, and began a new correspondence that influenced Newton to think about planetary motion. Hooke asked Newton about the trajectory a body would take falling to the Earth. Newton proposed an experiment to address the problem, but he made a mistake and suggested the trajectory would carve out a spiral path. Hooke subjected Newton's mistake to intense criticism, and this apparently drove Newton to work on the problem of planetary motion and the inverse square law of gravitational attraction.

Meanwhile, other leading intellects at the time, such as Edmund Halley (the discoverer of the famous comet) were working unsuccessfully on the problem of planetary motion. Halley made a famous trip to Cambridge in the summer of 1684 to seek Newton's advice on the problem. Newton answered immediately that he already calculated that a planet's motion around the sun takes the path of an ellipse, but he could not find the paper on which he had done the calculations. Eventually he sent the proof, along with some other calculations, to Halley in London. Halley was so impressed that he offered to pay to have Newton's work published. Newton went to work fine-tuning the details of his mathematical physics, and the result was the publication in 1687 of the now famous *Philosophia Naturalis Principia Mathematica – The Mathematical Principles of Natural Philosophy* (hereafter, *'Principia'*). In this work, Newton demonstrated a number of important things, including his three laws of motion, as well as the theory of gravitation. Some have argued that the *Principia* is the most important work in the history of intellectual thought.

Newton was launched pretty quickly into the public eye after the publication of the *Principia*. In 1696, he became Warden of the Mint, and then in 1700 he became Master of the Mint. This position gave him an extraordinary amount of power and money, as he was not only in charge of managing the treasury, but also in charge of bringing counterfeiters to justice. In 1703, after the death of Hooke, Newton became president of the Royal Society. In 1704 he was knighted by Queen Anne, and this is the same year that the first edition of his other major work, *Opticks,* was published. The *Opticks* was the culmination of his life-long work in this field, and dealt extensively with a corpuscular theory of light. Newton made a number of new editions of the *Principia* and the *Opticks* throughout the remainder of his life. He died in March 1727, and was given a grand funeral ceremony. He is buried in Westminster Abbey.

Although he was clearly an empiricist, his theory of universal gravitation would force many of his contemporary empiricists, such as Locke, to reconsider their philosophical views, especially their views concerning the status of mechanism. As we shall see, he cast doubt on the mechanist claim that matter is fundamentally inert. Although he did not offer a full epistemological theory of the sort given to us by Locke, he did present the 'Rules for the Study of Natural Philosophy' in the *Principia.* These were intended in large part to dictate the proper way to gain knowledge of nature.

7.1. THE NATURAL REALM: NEWTON'S *PRINCIPIA*

Recall the Aristotelian worldview (cf. Chapter 1, Section 1.2.2): the Earth stood in the centre of the universe, and the celestial spheres revolved around it. Nature was composed of hylomorphic substances, consisting of matter and form. The matter was purely passive, while form was active, and form is what gave matter powers to act. These forms were embedded in matter and they were goal-driven: it is in virtue of its form that the acorn has the goal or purpose of becoming an oak, and that is why it falls to the ground and sprouts. Everything was explained in terms of these hylomorphic substances using the framework of the 'four causes', and it was generally accepted that bodies had internal powers (forms).

Through the work of Copernicus, Galileo and others, the Aristotelian cosmology was gradually overturned in favour of the heliocentric system. Through the work of Bacon, Hobbes and others, the Scholastic view of nature was overturned in favour of a mechanistic outlook. Indeed, several of the classical empiricists, as we have seen, envisioned the world to be machine-like: it is fundamentally an aggregate of hunks of matter being pushed around by transfers of motion. Boyle, for example, explicitly compared nature to the clock at Strasbourg Cathedral in order to illustrate his mechanistic conception of the world, one in which everything occurs *via* the size, shape and motion of matter (cf. Chapter 5, Section 5.1.1).

But despite the revolutionary progress that took place during the transition from Aristotelianism to mechanism, there were still a number of philosophical difficulties. For example, Locke openly admitted that it is something of a mystery how the mechanical properties of matter cause sensory ideas (cf. Chapter 6, Section 6.1.3). In general, there did not seem to be many cases of successful mechanistic explanations aside from token examples involving clocks and keys (cf. Chapter 5, Section 5.1). And as we noted in the last chapter (cf. Chapter 6, Section 6.1.4), there was far from unanimous agreement about the cause of worldly motion.

Newton's *Principia* was nothing short of revolutionary, and it raised new philosophical problems. It forced people to see the universe from one perspective as something that can be captured by fairly simple mathematics, yet from another as far more complex than had been supposed by Aristotelians and mechanists alike. On the one hand, it completed the image of the universe as machine-like, as Newton showed it was capable of being largely captured by a few and elegant mathematical laws. This, of course, was quite in harmony with the mechanistic worldview. But on the other hand, it raised serious philosophical questions that frustrated both Newton and the mechanist movement. This is particularly true with respect to the notion of power, or force, and its connection with action at a distance.

7.1.1. A world of forces: universal gravitation

For our purposes, Newton's most important accomplishment is his theory of universal gravitation. As we have seen, the Scholastic Aristotelians believed that bodies had forms in them that endowed them with goal-directed powers (cf. Chapter 1, Section 1.2.3). Gassendi believed that material atoms were inherently active (Chapter 4, Section 4.1.1), and Boyle believed that matter was intrinsically inert, that God added motion to matter at creation, and that all subsequent activity was the result of the transfer of that motion (cf. Chapter 5, Section 5.1.1). For Locke, matter does not have active powers, since it cannot move itself (cf. Chapter 6, Section 6.1.4).

But according to Newton's theory of universal gravitation, every particle of matter in the universe attracts every other particle of matter. That is, the Newtonian world consists of forces in all bodies – active powers in all bodies – acting outwardly on all other bodies. Specifically, (a) every body in the universe attracts others with a force that is proportional to the products of their masses, and (b) inversely proportional to the square of the distance between those bodies. How should we understand this when it comes to everyday phenomena?

Focusing on (a) and (b), gravity is a mutually attractive force between any two objects. According to (a), the more massive an object, the greater is its force of attraction. Thus, when one releases a tennis ball, the tennis ball and the Earth are attracted to each other. However, since the Earth is far more massive than the tennis ball, it exerts a much greater force on the tennis ball than the tennis ball does on the Earth. Indeed, the tennis ball has virtually no pull on the Earth due to the relative difference in mass between the two objects. On the other hand, the Earth is pulled to the Sun since the Sun has far greater mass than the Earth.

According to (b), the force of attraction is inversely proportional to the square of the distance between any two objects. Thus, the farther away two objects are from each other, the less is the attractive force of gravity. The closer two objects are to each other, the greater is the attractive force. If the tennis ball were released far enough away from the Earth, the Earth would not cause it to fall to the Earth. But when one releases the tennis ball on a tennis court, the tennis ball is so close to the Earth that it is immediately brought to the Earth's surface.

In a nutshell, that is Newton's famous theory of universal gravitation. He finally stated the theory (though in abbreviated form) in Proposition 7 of Book 3 of the *Principia*: 'Gravity exists in all bodies universally, and is proportional to the quantity of matter in each'. So stated, it raised a host of philosophical questions, for Newton seems to have postulated an active power *in* bodies. To many, this seemed like a retreat to the doctrine of Scholastic forms, a doctrine the empiricists worked hard to overturn. *Is* it a retreat to Scholasticism? If not, what is gravity? In what sense does it exist 'in' bodies? Can it be explained mechanically? These are the questions that concerned the empiricists.

7.1.2. What kind of quality is gravity?

In the years following the publication of the *Principia*, it became increasingly clear that Newton's mathematical description of the behaviour of objects under the influence of gravity was right on target. However, despite Newton's success at giving *mathematical descriptions* of the behaviour of bodies, he was under pressure to explain the *very property* (or *quality*) of gravity itself. He showed that gravity 'exists *in* all bodies'. But what could this mean?

To bring the problem into sharper focus, consider Locke's primary qualities: shape, texture, mobility and so on. Each of these is an observable feature of bodies (at least, at the macroscopic level). But although the *effects* of gravity are observable – namely, the motion of bodies acted on by gravity – the force of gravity *itself* is not directly observable. Moreover, gravity does not seem to be something that can be deduced from purely mechanical qualities. That is, it does not seem as though the mere properties of size, shape, texture and so on *cause* mutual attraction. And so, two related philosophical questions presented themselves shortly after the publication of the *Principia:* what kind of quality is gravity? And what is the *cause* of gravity?

To begin, Newton refrained in several places from the claim that gravity is an 'essential' or 'innate' or 'inherent' property of matter. In a famous letter to then Trinity Headmaster, Richard Bentley, Newton explicitly denied that gravity is essential to matter:

> You sometimes speak of gravity as essential and inherent to matter. Pray do not ascribe that notion to me; for the cause of gravity is what I do not pretend to know, and therefore would take more time to consider of it. (Janiak, 100)

While we cannot be absolutely certain what Newton had in mind by the terms 'essential' and 'inherent', an *essential property* of some entity X is typically understood as a property of X that serves as a defining characteristic of X in such a way that X could not exist without that property. Thus, the property of being unmarried is an essential property of being a bachelor: one cannot be a married bachelor. According to some, extension is an essential property of matter: matter cannot exist without being extended in space. So, Newton's claim seems to be the claim that gravity is not essential to matter since matter could conceivably exist without gravity. It should also be noted that in this letter, Newton confessed that he did not know the cause of gravity. Perhaps if he knew the cause of gravity, then he would know whether it was essential or inherent to matter.

In another passage from the *Principia,* Newton suggests a specific reason why he believes that gravity cannot be essential to matter:

> [I]t will have to be concluded . . . that all bodies gravitate toward one another. . . . Yet I am by no means affirming that gravity is essential to bodies. By inherent force I mean only the force of inertia. This is immutable. Gravity is diminished as bodies recede from the Earth. (Janiak, 88f.)

In this passage, Newton contrasts a body's 'force of inertia', which we may think of as a body's mass, as Newton seems to have done, with the force of gravity. He claimed that the force of inertia is 'immutable': it remains with a given body under any conditions. On the other hand, gravity 'diminishes' when it moves away from the Earth. The point seems to be that gravity can 'disappear' from a hunk of matter under certain conditions. Specifically, under the condition that a given object is not near any other objects – consider a world with only one object – it will not have any gravity. Gravity is a *mutually* attractive force. If there is no other body around, there is no gravity. Thus, gravity can be separated from body, and is not essential to it.

It is worth noting in passing that this argument also rules out that gravity could be a primary quality of bodies. (However, Roger Cotes, the editor of the second edition of the *Principia* and author of its preface, seems clearly to suggest in the preface that gravity is a primary quality of bodies [cf. Janiak, 51]). Recall that Locke characterized primary qualities as those that are inseparable from body, or those that a body retains under any conditions or changes (cf. Chapter 6, Section 6.1.3). Locke cited solidity, texture and others as primary qualities since no matter what happens to a given object, it will always have these properties. But gravity, as we have just seen, *is* separable from body under certain conditions. Thus, it cannot be characterized as a primary quality. And it surely cannot be labelled a secondary quality, for the latter is understood as caused by mechanical primary qualities. But Newton conceded, as we have seen, that the cause of gravity is unknown.

Finally, Newton seems to have also conceded that whatever the cause of gravity, it is not a mechanical cause. Consider the following from the end of the *Principia:*

Thus far I have explained the phenomena of the heavens and of our sea by the force of gravity, but I have not yet assigned a cause to gravity. Indeed, this force arises from some cause that penetrates as far as the centres of the sun and planets without any diminution of its power to act, and that acts not in proportion to the quantity of the *surfaces* of the particles on which it acts (*as mechanical causes are wont to do*) but in proportion to the quantity of *solid* matter, and whose action is extended everywhere to immense distances, always decreasing as the squares of the distances. (Janiak, 92; some emphasis added)

In this passage, Newton argued that the cause of gravity could not be mechanical since mechanical causes appeal only to 'surface' properties such as texture and shape. Such properties seem irrelevant to gravity, which depends instead on the 'quantity of solid matter', the mass of a body. Thus, the most fundamental force in the universe does not yield to mechanistic explanation, as previous empiricists had hoped.

Newton's reluctance to specify the cause of gravity led many to accuse him of introducing unintelligible qualities into natural philosophy. His rationalist rival, Gottfried Leibniz, accused Newton of introducing gravity as a perpetual miracle, since it is not something that can be understood as coming from the nature of bodily matter. Others simply accused Newton of introducing an *occult quality*. Different philosophers had a different understanding of the meaning of 'occult' quality, but it suffices for our purposes to note that this negative accusation amounted to the charge that gravity, as a physical postulate, is unintelligible and explains nothing. The Aristotelians were frequently accused of positing occult qualities when it comes to forms, since the latter appear to be hidden unintelligible causes. Newton denied the charge of positing occult qualities in Query 31 of *Opticks,* where he explicitly contrasted his work with the Aristotelian tradition:

> And the Aristotelians gave the name of occult qualities, not to manifest qualities, but to such qualities only as they supposed to lie hid in bodies, and to be the unknown causes of manifest effects: such as would be the cause of gravity . . . if we should suppose that [this] force or action arose from qualities unknown to us, and incapable of being discovered or made manifest. Such occult qualities put a stop to the improvement of natural philosophy, and therefore of late years have been rejected. To tell us that every species of things is endowed with an occult specific quality by which it acts and produces manifest effects, is to tell us nothing: but to derive two or three general principles of motion from phenomena, and afterwards to tell us how the properties and actions of all corporeal things follow from those manifest principles, would be a very great step in philosophy, though the causes of those principles were not yet discovered. (Janiak, 137)

In this passage, Newton defended himself against the occult quality charge by distinguishing gravity from what he took to be problematic about Aristotelian occult qualities. First, unlike Aristotelian occult qualities – and here, Newton clearly has substantial forms in mind – the cause of gravity is still capable of discovery. Second, Aristotelian forms are occult because they explain nothing: they posit a 'specific' form for each object in order to account for that object's behaviour. The acorn acts as it does because it has the form of acorn, while the rose acts as it does because it has the quite different form of rose. This treatment of forms is explanatorily useless. On the other hand, to lay down *general* principles for the behaviour of motion, and show how the behaviour of *all* objects is explained by them is not explanatorily useless at all – *even if* we do not yet know the cause of those principles (such as the principle gravity).

In the end, then, Newton attempted to walk a tightrope: he confessed that the cause of gravity is – at least temporarily – a mystery. Yet he also insisted that it is not occult, but is explanatorily fruitful. Indeed, in this very context near the end of the *Principia,* he delivered his famous line about not engaging in speculative hypotheses about the cause of gravity: 'I have not yet been able to deduce from phenomena the reason for these properties of gravity, and I do not feign [i.e. frame] hypotheses' (Janiak, 92).

7.1.3. Mechanism and action at a distance

Recall that it is a central belief of all the empiricists covered thus far that all causal relations must occur through mechanical impact, or 'impulse' (cf. Chapter 3, Section 3.1.1 and Chapter 6, Section 6.1.3). In other words, there can be no *action at a distance*. The reason this was a fundamental belief of the empiricists is not difficult to see. Suppose someone asked you to lift a desk. Suppose further that person asked you to do it without touching the desk, and without using any other instruments to touch the desk. You would naturally think that such a thing could not be done. Why? Because it is *impossible* to lift the desk without any *impact* on it. In other words, to do so would involve performing an *action* on the desk at a *distance* from it. This is what is called 'action at a distance'.

Newton's theory of universal gravitation, in addition to raising questions about what kind of quality gravity is, also seemed to involve action at a distance. This is important not simply because action at a distance seems mysterious, perhaps even impossible, but also because it violated the mechanist maxim that all action must occur through causal impact. Every empiricist prior to Newton explained everything, even sensation, in terms of mechanical impact, and did so even when it was unclear how this kind of impact could possibly cause such things as ideas in the mind.

As we have seen, Newton refrained from claiming that gravity was essential to matter, and we have seen some reasons why he did so. Interestingly, the issue of whether gravity was innate to matter was connected in Newton's mind with the problem of action at a distance. This is abundantly clear in a letter to Bentley:

It is inconceivable that inanimate brute matter should, without the mediation of something else, which is not material, operate upon and affect other matter without mutual contact, as it must be, if gravitation . . . be essential and inherent in it. And this is one reason why I desired you would not ascribe innate gravity to me. That gravity should be innate, inherent, and essential to matter, so that one body may act upon another at a distance through a vacuum without the mediation of anything else, by and through which their action and force may be conveyed from one to another, is to me so great an absurdity, that I believe no man who has in philosophical matters a competent faculty of thinking can ever fall into it. Gravity must be caused by an agent acting constantly according to certain laws; but whether this agent be material or immaterial, I have left to the consideration of my readers. (Janiak, 102f.)

Note that Newton here claimed that one of the very *reasons* that he refrained from claiming that gravity is inherent to matter is because it implies action at a distance. Apparently, according to Newton, to say that gravity is essential to matter is to commit oneself to action at a distance. In this case, the action involves the attraction of bodies to each other over a distance: the Earth, *via* the force of attraction, *causes* the moon to rotate in its orbit at a distance. *But it makes no contact with the moon.* Clearly, Newton believed that action at a distance is unintelligible, especially when it is held to occur through a vacuum, a place devoid of matter, as outer space appeared to be, for a vacuum has no matter through which there could be causal transmissions. In short, if there is no matter between the planets, how could one planet act on another as Newton claimed?

Newton offered no answer, and he regarded this an issue for future research at the same time that some of his contemporaries accused him of positing perpetual miracles and occult qualities. The crucial point for our purposes is that with the work of Newton, the mechanist viewpoint began to decline dramatically. The world is not fundamentally mechanical in the Hobbes/Boyle/Locke sense. Objects appear to act upon one another over vast distances and they do not appear to do so in virtue of any mechanical properties. Thus, despite the extremely important success of Newton's *Principia*, it raised deep and perplexing philosophical issues, and was a major contributor to the decline of the popularity of mechanism.

7.2. KNOWLEDGE AND EXPERIENCE: RULES FOR THE STUDY OF NATURAL PHILOSOPHY

In the third edition of the *Principia*, Newton presented his famous four 'Rules for the Study of Natural Philosophy'. (He presented rules in the first two editions, but there were fewer rules in those earlier editions.) These rules are not exactly a statement of method akin to the detailed methods left to us by Bacon and Hobbes, nor are they indicative of a worked out epistemological theory. But they did underlie Newton's thinking about the proper way to attain knowledge of nature. As we shall see in Section 7.2.2, they may also have played a part in the beginning of the separation between philosophy and natural science.

7.2.1. The four rules

The first rule is:

Rule 1: *No more causes of natural things should be admitted than are both true and sufficient to explain their phenomena.* (Janiak, 87)

This rule reflects Newton's preference for explanatory simplicity in the quest for knowledge, as it dictates that one should not invoke more causes of natural things than are necessary to explain those natural things. Some commentators have noted that this rule may not be independent of Newton's religious belief that God would create an orderly universe with a high degree of explanatory simplicity. In any event, contemporary philosophers of science often cite simplicity as an explanatory virtue.

The second rule is:

Rule 2: *Therefore, the causes assigned to natural effects of the same kind must be, so far as possible, the same.* (Janiak, 87)

In other words, if two effects are the same, then we may presume that the causes are the same as well. This is a type of reasoning by analogy: if Jones is wincing and holding his arm, and we discover that the cause of Jones's pain is a broken arm, we should conclude that the cause of similar behaviour in Smith is also a broken arm. Newton cites as one example 'the falling of stones in Europe and America', about which we ought to conclude the causes (gravity) are the same. This type of reasoning, famously captured in slogans such as 'like effects prove like causes', is often successful but it is notoriously invalid, and Newton does not claim it as a guarantor of truth.

Rule three is:

Rule 3: *Those qualities of bodies that cannot be intended and remitted [i.e. increased and diminished] and that belong to all bodies on which experiments can be made should be taken as qualities of all bodies universally.* (Janiak, 87)

This rule perhaps more than any other reflects Newton's empiricism. In his discussion of the rule, he emphasizes repeatedly that we must begin our knowledge of nature with sensory observation, and we must not posit any entities that lack such an empirical basis. But the main point of the rule is that one should conclude that whatever unchangeable qualities are found in objects as a result of direct observation (experiment) are found in *all* objects. More specifically, this rule holds with respect to qualities 'that cannot be intended and remitted' – that is, qualities that are inseparable from objects, such as Locke's primary qualities, but unlike for example, colour. Thus, we ought to conclude that celestial matter has the same qualities as the terrestrial matter we find on Earth. For example, by observation we see that all matter is extended, impenetrable, and endowed with a force of gravity, and none of these qualities can be separated from matter. Thus, we have reason to conclude that the matter in outer space also has these qualities. Indeed, Newton and others appealed to this rule in support of *universal* gravitation, or the idea that *all* objects, even those beyond the reach of our experiments, gravitate.

Finally, rule four is:

Rule 4: *In experimental philosophy, propositions gathered from phenomena by induction should be considered either exactly or very nearly true notwithstanding any contrary hypotheses, until yet other phenomena make such propositions either more exact or liable to exceptions.* (Janiak, 89)

This rule is, of course, reminiscent of Bacon, who was the first to present a detailed method of induction (cf. Chapter 2, Section 2.2). Notice that Newton's rule is carefully written: induction 'should be considered' as delivering truth, but it does not guarantee such knowledge. Indeed, the rule clearly makes room for revisions of propositions concluded from induction, and clearly reflects his empiricism. It mandates that knowledge of the natural world is to be had only by sensory observation of phenomena, and the conclusions drawn from that observation can only be revised or overturned by 'other phenomena' observed by the senses. As he remarked in his comments on the rule, conclusions based on induction are not to be 'nullified by hypotheses' that are not founded in empirical observation.

7.2.2. Whither natural philosophy?

Newton is almost always referred to as a physicist or a mathematician. And he certainly was both of these things. But it is also true that he was a philosopher, although we rarely hear him labelled as such. This is somewhat unfortunate, since he labelled himself a philosopher. After all, the full title of his masterpiece is *The Mathematical Principles of Natural Philosophy*. And in that work he offered philosophical arguments for the existence of God based on the work he had done: 'This most elegant system of the sun, planets, and comets could not have arisen without the design and dominion of an intelligent and powerful being' (Janiak, 90). The *Principia* also contains a number of speculations about the relationship between God and universal space, and an endorsement of final causes. Moreover, in the *Opticks,* he suggested that natural philosophy yields knowledge of the 'first cause', God: 'And though every true step made in this philosophy brings us not immediately to the knowledge of the first cause, yet it brings us nearer to it, and on that account is to be highly valued' (Janiak, 130). Passages such as this leave the impression that Newton believed his study of the universe *just was* a study of the ways of the divine mind.

Thus, Newton's work contains much that is of interest to the philosopher. But that having been noted, his 'Rules' discussed above do suggest the beginning of a split between traditional philosophy and natural science. Prior to Newton, there was no clear division between science, religion and philosophy, and indeed it was not until much later after Newton that we see these divisions fully demarcated. As we have seen, one theme throughout the 'Rules' is the emphasis on observation and induction, and these are, of course, methods today most closely related to the natural sciences. Of course, philosophers use induction and observation as well, but they are also interested in more traditional metaphysical topics, which Newton here seems to bracket away from natural science.

7.3. CONCLUSION: NEWTON THE EMPIRICIST

It is well known that Newton's work was revolutionary. But it seems not as well known that Newton was an empiricist who worked with Boyle and Locke, and eventually had a profound influence over the empiricist movement. As an empiricist, he insisted, as did Locke and others, that knowledge of nature is founded on sensory observation, and experimentation in particular. He showed that through observation we could describe the behaviour of objects with fairly simple mathematical laws. He also showed that through empirical observation, we could extend our knowledge to *all* bodies generally.

But his work also revolutionized the empiricist movement itself. Up until Newton, classical empiricists generally believed that the concept of mechanism was the means to acquiring additional knowledge of nature. Newton presented the mechanist movement with a much more complex universe, one filled with forces as opposed to merely mechanistic properties of inert matter. In doing so, he showed that mechanism could not go very far toward explaining the behaviour of objects, as Hobbes, Gassendi, Boyle and Locke had hoped.

He also left the movement with some perplexing philosophical problems involving the cause of gravitational force, and its seeming ability to cause action at a distance. But as we shall see in the next chapter, these are perplexing issues only under a certain interpretation of the role of science. Berkeley had a view of science that he believed solved some of the issues raised by Newton's work.

CHAPTER 8

GEORGE BERKELEY (1685–1753)

George Berkeley was born on 12 March 1685 near Kilkenny, Ireland. He was born five years before the publication of Locke's *Essay Concerning Human Understanding,* and only two years before the publication of Newton's *Principia.* He had thoughtful reactions to both works, as he either rejected or reinterpreted central thoughts of Locke and Newton. He wrote on many topics: philosophy, economics, medicine and theories of vision, among others. He is best known for endorsing *idealism,* the (strange?) view that matter does not exist, and the only things that do exist are minds and their ideas. Curiously, he touted his idealism as the best *defence* of common sense.

At age 15, Berkeley entered Trinity College, Dublin, and he graduated in 1704 at age 19. Compared to the education received by earlier empiricists, Berkeley's formal education was modern. He learned about Descartes and other thinkers associated with the new philosophy, and the curriculum was in general anti-Aristotelian. Three years after graduating from Trinity, Berkeley became a fellow there, and shortly thereafter was ordained a priest in the Anglican Church. He remained associated with Trinity until 1724.

During this time at Trinity, Berkeley was prolific as he published his most famous works. In 1709, he published his *Essay Towards a New Theory of Vision* and only a year later (1710) he published *A Treatise Concerning the Principles of Human Knowledge* (hereafter, '*Principles*'). This latter work is important for our purposes since it contains concise arguments for his immaterialist worldview. In 1713, he published *Three Dialogues Between Hylas and Philonous,* a work intended to expand upon the philosophy presented in the *Principles,* and one that was targeted for a more popular audience.

This chapter focuses mostly on these two latter works. By the time these books were published – and they are his most famous works – Berkeley was only 28 years old.

In 1716 Berkeley took an extended tour of Europe as a chaperone and tutor of the son of the provost of Trinity. It was during this time that Berkeley wrote a tract in the philosophy of science and one especially relevant to Newtonian mechanics. The work, *De Motu* ('On Motion') was published in Latin in 1721, just after his return to England. That same year he was awarded a Doctor of Divinity in Dublin, and only three years later (1724) he was appointed the Anglican Dean of Derry. Around this time, Berkeley began to devise a plan for which he would become somewhat famous.

The plan was to build a college in Bermuda for Native Americans and sons of settlers. At least part of his motivation was that Berkeley felt that Britain was in spiritual decay. Just before formulating the plan, Berkeley published *An Essay Towards Preventing the Ruin of Great Britain,* an essay that expressed his view that society in Britain had been corrupted. He lobbied persistently for the money to found the college, and was successful at securing pledges from private donors as well as pledges from Parliament. After marrying Anne Forster in August of 1728, Berkeley and his bride sailed to America only a month later. He settled in Newport, Rhode Island, and built a house there named Whitehall, which is still standing today. Sadly, political support for the college fell through and after three years in America, the money still had not arrived. Berkeley and his family donated the books intended for the college to Yale University, and returned to London.

In 1734 Berkeley was consecrated Bishop of Cloyne and he returned to Ireland to live in that diocese. By all accounts, Berkeley was a good bishop for the next 18 years, always looking to better society and human welfare. In 1744, he published *Siris,* a work primarily concerned with the healing powers of tar water (a liquid formed by boiling the tar of pine trees in water). Berkeley discovered tar water in America, and argued that it was effective in curing a host of ailments. It is by far the strangest of Berkeley's works, yet it was in his own lifetime his most popular and best-selling book. In 1752 Berkeley moved again to be near his son who was studying in Oxford. He died somewhat suddenly a year later at the age of 68.

Berkeley did not gain philosophical fame because of a general agreement with his philosophy. On the contrary, most people found his immaterialism completely implausible. But many of those same people have, or have had a difficult time stating exactly what was wrong with his views. His most valuable contributions to the empiricist movement were his concise straightforward arguments designed to rid the empiricist movement of certain philosophical hurdles, especially those hurdles he believed were set up by Locke. Berkeley's work became famous because it forced other thinkers to reconsider their own views, not because they found Berkeley's final philosophy attractive in the way in which, for example, many found the work of Locke and Newton attractive. We shall take a close look at his criticisms of some standard empiricist doctrines, as well as the empiricist philosophy he offered.

8.1. THE NATURAL REALM: BERKELEY'S IDEALISM

Berkeley is best known for his idealism. This is an immaterialist worldview, one that implies that there is no such thing as an external world of matter. It is surely a counterintuitive philosophy, one that is downright perplexing. But it is also, I believe, frequently misunderstood. In what follows, we will begin with Berkeley's worldview and then take a critical look at his specific arguments for it.

8.1.1. The world contains only souls and ideas

Although it is true that Berkeley's idealism implies that there is no such thing as an external world of bodies, this view must not be confused with the view that ordinary objects do not exist, for Berkeley certainly believed ordinary objects do exist. Indeed, as we shall see later, Berkeley believed that his idealism was the way to *avoid* scepticism about ordinary objects. This is partly evident in the opening section of the *Principles:*

It is evident to anyone who takes a survey of the objects of human knowledge, that they are either ideas actually imprinted on the senses, or else such as are perceived by attending to the passions and operations of the mind, or lastly ideas formed by help of memory or imagination . . . And as several of these are observed to accompany each other, they come to be marked by one name, and so to be reputed as one thing. Thus, for example, a certain color taste, smell, figure and consistence having been observed to go together, are accounted one distinct thing, signified by the name *apple*. (*Principles* §1)

Clearly, Berkeley believed in a world of ordinary objects. In this passage, he arrived at that conclusion by putting forth the 'evident' thesis that knowledge is concerned exclusively with ideas, all of which are rooted in sensory experience. This, of course, is exactly the thesis Locke and others put forth (cf. Chapter 6, Sections 6.1.2 and 6.2), and it is the thesis that unites the empiricist camp. But it may be the only point of agreement between Berkeley and earlier empiricists, for Berkeley *identifies* ideas with objects: the 'apple' *just is* a collection of sensory ideas (e.g. the idea of red, round, smooth, tart etc.). Locke, as have seen, believed that our sensory idea of an apple *represents* a mind-independent hunk of matter (i.e. an apple). But in the above passage from Berkeley, there is no reference at all to an underlying mind-independent substance that gives us such ideas; there is no material substrate in which these sensory ideas inhere. Apples and chairs – ordinary objects – do indeed exist, but they *just are* collections of ideas.

So, Berkeley believed that all bodies are *merely* collections of ideas, and there is no external world of matter. But there is more to the world than bundles of ideas:

But besides all that endless variety of ideas or objects of knowledge, there is likewise something which knows or perceives them, and exercises diverse operations, as willing, imagining, remembering about them. This perceiving, active being is what I call *mind, spirit, soul,* or *myself.* (*Principles* §2)

In addition to ideas, there are those things that perceive ideas: souls or spirits or minds, for example, humans. Berkeley believed we know immediately through introspection there are such things. Ideas are the passive objects of perception, and souls are active entities that perceive ideas and will themselves to do things. We now have the fundamentals of Berkeley's worldview. It consists of a dualism of mind and ideas, and nothing else.

But although Berkeley's worldview is adequately captured by the claim that there are only minds and bodies, this fails to underscore an important component to his thinking. Perhaps the best way to approach the issue is to ask where our ideas come from if there is no external world of objects? In other words, according to previous empiricists such as Hobbes, Locke and Boyle, what explains the fact that we have sensory ideas is the existence of a mind-independent world that *causes* our ideas *via* mechanical impact. But for Berkeley there is no mind-independent world to cause our ideas. Where then do our ideas come from?

Berkeley addressed this question in the *Principles* and it comes in the form of an argument for the existence of God. Given his idealism, there are only three candidates for the source of our ideas: (1) other ideas; (2) myself; (3) some spirit other than me. Berkeley ruled out the first candidate in Section 25 of the *Principles:*

All our ideas, sensations, or the things which we perceive, by whatsoever names they may be distinguished, are visibly inactive, there is nothing of power or agency included in them. So that one idea or object of thought cannot produce, or make any alteration in another. (*Principles* §25)

The cause of any one of my ideas cannot be another idea, according to Berkeley, since an idea is 'visibly inactive'. That is, as a passive object of perception, it does not have the power or force to be the cause of anything, other ideas included. An idea gets perceived, but it does not actively *do* anything.

But Berkeley rejected the second candidate too, for although I cause *some* of my ideas – for example, when I will myself to imagine a unicorn, or decide to conjure up a memory – my present sensory ideas are produced without my willing anything. They come to me involuntarily:

When in broad daylight I open my eyes, it is not in my power to choose whether I shall see or no, or to determine what particular objects shall present themselves to my view; and so likewise as to the hearing and other senses, the ideas imprinted on them are not creatures of my will. There is therefore some other will or spirit that produces them. (*Principles* §29)

Since sensory ideas come to me against my will, and since other ideas cannot cause these sensory ideas, it follows Berkeley argued, that 'some other will or spirit' causes them. Thus far, the conclusion is simply that some other spirit produces my ideas, not that it is God. But Berkeley argues that the fact that our sensory ideas come to us in an orderly law-like fashion that allows us to anticipate nature and organize our affairs (e.g. fire produces heat, food produces health etc.) shows that the spirit producing these ideas is powerful, wise and benevolent. Moreover, this spirit, in virtue of producing all sensory ideas, is literally the 'Author of Nature' – that is, God (*Principles* §§31–33).

In short, in Berkeley's universe, there are two types of entities, ideas and spirits. One of these spirits is God, the producer of the ideas that constitute natural objects. All other spirits are finite persons.

8.1.2. *Esse est percipi*: two arguments for idealism/immaterialism

Berkeley's worldview seems sharply at odds with common sense, and marks a radical turn in the empiricist movement. What led him to adopt such a view?

In fact, there are many considerations that led him to adopt immaterialism, and we shall see his cumulative case throughout this chapter. Many of his considerations turn on the fact that other empiricist views, such as Locke's, are plagued with difficulties that can only be overcome, according to Berkeley, by an idealist metaphysics. But at least two arguments stand out as being directly intended to show that there are no mind-independent hunks of matter.

(1) Against the 'Strangely Prevailing Opinion'. In the fourth section of the *Principles,* Berkeley presented his first argument against those who believe that objects exist outside of minds:

It is indeed an opinion strangely prevailing amongst men, that houses, mountains, rivers, and in a word all sensible objects have an existence natural or real, distinct from their being perceived by the understanding. But with how great an assurance and acquiescence soever this principle may be entertained in the world; yet whoever shall find in his heart to call it in question, may, if I mistake not, perceive it to involve a manifest contradiction. For what are the forementioned objects but the things we perceive by sense, and what do we perceive besides our own ideas or sensations; and is it not plainly repugnant that any one of these or any combination of them should exist unperceived? (*Principles* §4)

The argument presented here is brief and to the point:

(1) We perceive sensible objects such as houses, mountains and rivers.
(2) We only perceive sensible ideas, and ideas cannot exist outside of a mind.
(3) Thus, sensible objects such as houses, mountains and rivers *just are* sensible ideas and cannot exist outside of a mind.

In other words, as Berkeley often put it: *esse est percipi,* or *to be is to be perceived.*

It is difficult to dispute that the argument is logically tight, for the conclusion appears to follow if one accepts the premises. Clearly, the controversial premise here is (2), the claim that what we perceive are sensible ideas. But this is a premise that was accepted by many in Berkeley's time, and even today. Recall that Locke accepted it, for the claim that the objects of perception are ideas is one that is central to Locke's philosophy. But one might object to it in at least two ways.

First, one might simply deny that what we perceive are ideas, and maintain that we perceive mind-independent objects *directly.* Even for reasons aside from his idealism, this is not a claim that Berkeley would have accepted. For example, in the *Dialogues,* Berkeley drew upon the example of an oar with one end in the water, and argued that a person simply could not be mistaken about what she perceives, namely, a sensory *idea* of a bent oar, not an *actual* mind-independent bent oar. He also argued in the 'Third Dialogue' that the fact that colours appear differently under different conditions shows that colours are entirely mind-dependent – an argument reminiscent of Locke, who was not an idealist. Recall that Locke's arguments for the distinction between primary and secondary qualities seem to require that ideas are the immediate objects of perception (cf. Chapter 6, Section 6.1.2). At least, this is the case with respect to secondary qualities. Locke explicitly defined secondary qualities as powers to produce in us certain *ideas.* Thus, if one is in the grips of Locke's theory of qualities, one might be committed to the claim that ideas are the direct objects of perception. Many materialists would agree, and so the claim that ideas are the direct objects of perception can be defended independently of a commitment to idealism. In any event, we shall see that Berkeley's second argument, if successful, would militate against the claim that objects are perceived directly.

Second, one might concede that ideas are the objects of perception, but argue that material bodies are perceived *indirectly*. This would be a view closer to Locke's, who held that even though we perceive ideas directly, we perceive material bodies insofar as our ideas *represent* those bodies. That is, we perceive material bodies *through* our ideas, and so the conclusion that sensible ideas are to be *identified* with material bodies is unwarranted, for ideas are distinct entities from bodies.

This response amounts to an endorsement of indirect realism, or the representational theory of perception (cf. Chapter 6, Section 6.2.1). As we will see in the next section, Berkeley launched a full force attack against every component of this theory. Since it is primarily an epistemological theory concerning the mind's perceptual access to the world, it will be discussed in the context of Berkeley's epistemology in the next section. Note for now that Berkeley was armed to resist the representational theory of perception.

(2) The Master Argument. Whatever the merits of these two objections to Berkeley's first argument, they may not have bothered him much at all since he was prepared to rest his entire case on his so-called 'Master Argument' (as commentators continue to call it). This argument begins in Section 22 of the *Principles:*

> For to what purpose is it to dilate on that which may be demonstrated with the utmost evidence in a line or two, to anyone that is capable of the least reflection? It is but looking into your own thoughts, and so trying whether you can conceive it possible for a sound, or figure, or motion, or color, to exist without the mind, or unperceived. This easy trial may make you see, that what you contend for, is a downright contradiction. Insomuch that I am content to put the whole upon this issue; if you can but conceive it possible for one extended moveable substance . . . to exist otherwise than in a mind perceiving it, I shall readily give up the

cause. . . . I say, the bare possibility of your opinion's being true, shall pass for an argument that it is so. (*Principles* §22)

The argument here begins with Berkeley issuing a challenge: if one can even conceive that it is *possible* for a material object to exist unperceived, Berkeley would 'readily give up the case', and grant that there exist mind-independent material objects. So, one needs to conceive of an object existing in such a way that no one perceives it, that is, a conception of matter existing independently of a mind.

Despite how easy it might seem to meet this challenge, Berkeley believed the challenge cannot be met:

> But say you, surely there is nothing easier than to imagine trees, for instance, in a park, or books existing in a closet, and nobody by to perceive them. I answer, you may so, there is no difficulty in it: but what is all this, I beseech you, more than framing in your mind certain ideas which you call *books* and *trees,* and at the same time omitting to frame the idea of anyone that may perceive them? But do not you yourself perceive or think of them all the while? This therefore is nothing to the purpose . . . [I]t does not show that you can conceive it possible . . . [A] little attention will discover to anyone the truth and evidence of what is here said, and make it unnecessary to insist on any other proofs against the existence of material substance. (*Principles* §23)

In this passage, Berkeley completed the argument. His point was that it is *impossible* to conceive of an object existing unperceived, for the very moment you attempt to do so, *you* thereby think of and thus perceive that object. Thus, you are *not* conceiving of an object that exists unperceived, and to do so is impossible. Unperceived mind-independent objects are impossible. Again, *esse est percipi, or to be is to be perceived.*

Despite Berkeley's confidence that the entire case for immaterialism can rest on this argument alone, many commentators have pointed out what appears to be an obvious flaw in the argument. Berkeley seems to conflate the *act* of conceiving something with the *representational content* of what is conceived. When I conceive of a tree existing in a park unperceived, I do, of course, conceive of this state of affairs. But it does *not* follow that what I am conceiving is a tree that is *now* perceived by me. On the contrary, the very *content* of my conception is an *un*perceived tree. Thus, it *is* possible to conceive of an object existing unperceived, and so Berkeley's argument, it seems, fails.

Why did Berkeley find the Master Argument so compelling? It is difficult to see why, and I will not attempt to answer this question. While it is important to note that he was willing to rest so much of his case on this argument, it is equally important to note that there are many more considerations involved in his case against the existence of mind-independent material objects. One crucial consideration concerns his discussion of the primary–secondary quality distinction.

8.1.3. Against the primary/secondary quality distinction

Recall that for Locke there is a distinction to be drawn between primary and secondary qualities (cf. Chapter 6, Section 6.1.3). Primary qualities, such as size, shape and solidity are 'inseperable' qualities of bodies in the sense that bodies retain these qualities throughout any changes to them. Moreover, our ideas of primary qualities resemble those qualities in bodies. Secondary qualities, on the other hand, are not inherent in objects, for they are *powers of* the primary qualities to produce in us ideas of colours, sounds, tastes and so on. Our ideas of secondary qualities do not resemble the secondary qualities of bodies. The secondary qualities are mind-dependent, for tastes, colours and so on require a sensing mind for their occurrence.

Obviously, Berkeley did not believe in the existence of primary qualities understood as objectively inhering in external bodies, and it is clear that he took the two arguments in the previous section to have ruled them out. But recall that Locke argued that we have good grounds for drawing a *distinction* between the two types of qualities. At least part of the reason centres on the idea that secondary qualities seem to be mind-dependent and primary qualities do not seem to be mind-dependent. If Locke were correct that a distinction along these lines can be drawn, then we might have at least some reason for thinking that there are mind-independent qualities, that is, primary qualities of external bodies.

Berkeley believed that the initial attractiveness of Locke's doctrine rests on a significant oversight. In several passages in the *Principles*,

Berkeley argued explicitly against the *distinction* between primary and secondary qualities:

> Now if it be certain, that those [primary] qualities are insepar- ably united with the other sensible qualities, and not, even in thought, capable of being abstracted from them, it plainly fol- lows that they exist only in the mind. But I desire anyone to reflect and try, whether he can by any abstraction of thought, conceive the extension and motion of a body, without all other sensible qualities. For my own part, I see evidently that it is not in my power to frame an idea of a body extended and moved, but I must withal give it some color or other sensible quality which is acknowledged to exist only in the mind. In short, exten- sion, figure, and motion, abstracted from all other qualities, are inconceivable. Where therefore the other sensible qualities are, there must these be also, to wit, in the mind and nowhere else. (*Principles* §10)

The reasoning in this passage is fairly straightforward: Locke and others make a distinction between primary and secondary qualities according to which the latter exist in the mind and the former do not. But we cannot even conceive of an extended body (primary qualities) existing totally devoid of any colour (secondary quality). Thus, since colours are clearly mind-dependent (as Locke showed – see previous section), extension, shape and motion must also be mind-dependent, since these latter qualities cannot be conceived as 'stripped down' of their secondary qualities, such as colour. We simply cannot conceive of a body devoid of any colour whatsoever. Thus, there is no basis for a distinction between primary and sec- ondary qualities: if one of them is mind-dependent, so is the other. Secondary qualities are mind-dependent; hence, so are primary qualities.

After presenting this argument against the *grounds of the dis- tinction* between primary and secondary qualities, Berkeley changed strategies and argued that every consideration that leads one to believe that secondary qualities are mind-dependent also leads one to believe that primary qualities are mind-dependent. For example, just as the appearance of colours depends on the conditions under which they are observed, so too texture, shape and motion also appear differently depending on the conditions under which they are observed. A 'smooth' table will appear 'rough' when observed under a microscope, and a single object will appear to have different shapes depending on one's perspective. 'In short', Berkeley argued, 'let anyone consider those arguments, which are thought manifestly to prove that colors and tastes exist only in the mind, and he shall find they may with equal force, be brought to prove the same thing of extension, figure, and motion' (*Principles* §15).

Berkeley was not only one of the earliest critics of the primary–secondary quality distinction, for he may also have been one of its sharpest critics. Since the time of Berkeley, philosophers have debated whether any meaningful distinction can be drawn between the two types of qualities. It seems clear that even if one is not persuaded by Berkeley's direct arguments for immaterialism, it must be conceded that his criticisms of the Lockean materialist view, a view rooted in a distinction between primary and secondary qualities, have succeeded in forcing a reconsideration of the distinction, a distinction whose basis may now seem perplexing.

8.2. KNOWLEDGE AND EXPERIENCE: BERKELEY'S COMMON SENSE EPISTEMOLOGY

As odd as it may seem, Berkeley touted his philosophy as one based on common sense, and as the only antidote to scepticism. He clearly believed that the representational theory of perception ('indirect realism') invited scepticism, and he may be correct about this (cf. Chapter 6, Section 6.2.1). In this section, I discuss first his attack on the representational theory of perception (or 'indirect realism'), and then turn to his positive programme, including the reasons why Berkeley believed that his philosophy was the product of common sense.

8.2.1. Against the representational theory of perception

Berkeley's attack on the representational theory of perception is systematic, for he attacks every component of the theory previously laid out in Chapter 6, Section 6.2.1. Nearly every early modern empiricist prior to Berkeley adopted the theory, but it is most clearly articulated in Locke. Recall that this theory has four components: (1) The Causal Component;

(2) The Resemblance Component; (3) The Indirect Component; (4) The Realist Component. I briefly consider each in light of Berkeley's critique.

1. The Causal Component: Recall that according to Locke, the primary qualities of bodies *cause* ideas in the human mind. That is, ordinary objects *causally impact* our senses, *via* imperceptible bits of matter, and this in turn causes ideas in our mind.

Berkeley's attack on this component focuses on the explanatory impotence of the causal component. That is, the causal component is often adopted a means of *explaining* why we have sensory perceptions. Surely it is natural to assume that the best explanation of why I presently have a sensory perception of a computer is because there exists an enduring mind-independent object (a computer) in front of me that *causes* me to have this perception. Berkeley argued that this assumption explains nothing:

> [F]or though we give the materialists their external bodies, they by their own confession are never the nearer knowing how our ideas are produced: since they own themselves unable to comprehend in what manner body can act upon spirit, or how it is possible that it should imprint any idea in the mind. Hence it is evident the production of ideas or sensations in our minds, can be no reason why we should suppose matter or corporeal substances, since that is acknowledged to remain equally inexplicable with, or without this supposition. (*Principles* §19)

It is true that even Locke admitted that it is something of a mystery how material qualities produce ideas in us (cf. *Essay* II, 8, §13, and Chapter 6, Section 6.1.3). The difficulty is that mind-independent material objects are entirely different in kind from non-material ideas: how can something with extension, shape, size and motion produce something (an idea) that is neither extended, nor with shape, nor size, nor motion? In this passage, Berkeley argued that, contrary to what one might suppose, the supposition that there exist mind-independent material objects cannot explain why we have the ideas we do; simply stating that objects 'cause' ideas is not enlightening, for we want to know *how* ideas get produced. Thus, materialism explains nothing, and the causal component is not well motivated.

2. The Resemblance Component: Recall that in his discussion of primary and secondary qualities, Locke committed himself to the 'resemblance thesis': our ideas of the primary qualities of bodies *resemble* those qualities in bodies.

Berkeley argued that such a claim is unwarranted:

> But say you, though the ideas themselves do not exist without the mind, yet there may be things like them whereof they are copies or resemblances, which things exist without the mind, in an unthinking substance. I answer, an idea can be like nothing but an idea; a color or figure can be like nothing but another color or figure. (*Principles* §8)

Berkeley's response was once again right to the point: an idea cannot resemble anything other than an idea. Why? There is some hint of an answer in what Berkeley wrote next. He followed this passage with the following challenge to the materialist: are the external objects – objects of which our ideas are resemblances – *themselves* perceivable? If the materialist answers 'yes', then they must be ideas, since as Berkeley and Locke and others have already argued (cf. Section 8.1.2 above), ideas are the only things perceivable; they are the immediate objects of perception. But if the materialist answers 'no' to the question of whether external objects are perceivable, then the materialist's claim that our ideas are resemblances of them is completely unfounded, for it amounts to the claim that our ideas resemble something 'invisible', 'intangible' and so on. (*Principles* §8). Thus, the resemblance component is at best unwarranted, and at worst simply false.

3. The Indirect Component: According to this component, mind-independent objects are perceived *indirectly:* I perceive external tables and chairs by perceiving ideas of them. Bear in mind that the indirect component, though closely related to the causal component, is different from it. The causal component is presented as an (efficient causal) *explanation* of the occurrence of our sensory ideas. The indirect component concedes that ideas are the immediate objects of perception, and in itself takes no stance on what explains the existence of our sensory ideas. It simply states that mind-independent objects in fact exist *and* are perceived indirectly.

Berkeley argued against this component by presenting two alternatives. If there are mind-independent external objects, then one can know this either through the senses, or by using reason:

As for our senses, by them we have the knowledge only of our sensations, ideas, or those things that are immediately perceived by sense, call them what you will: but they do not inform us that things exist without the mind, or unperceived, like to those which are perceived. This the materialists themselves acknowledge. It remains therefore that if we have any knowledge at all of external things, it must be by reason, inferring their existence from what is immediately perceived by sense. But what reason can induce us to believe the existence of bodies without the mind, from what we perceive, since the very patrons of matter themselves do not pretend, there is any necessary connection betwixt them and our ideas. (*Principles* §18)

Berkeley argued here that since the only things *directly* perceivable by the senses are ideas, the senses do not demonstrate the existence of external objects. Thus, it must be that we have reason to infer 'their existence from what is immediately perceived by sense', that is, it must be that we can reason to the conclusion that we perceive them *indirectly* from the ideas of sense. But this will not work, Berkeley argued, due to the fact that everyone will grant that there is no 'necessary connection' between external bodily qualities and our senses. In other words, since it is at least possible that I can have sensory ideas without the existence of external matter, and since we have no conception of how external bodies could produce ideas (per the attack on the causal component), we must admit that we have no grounds for claiming that we perceive external bodies indirectly either. Thus, the indirect component is at best unwarranted, and more likely simply false – or so Berkeley argued.

4. The Realism Component: This component maintains that bodies, or material objects, exist independently of perception. Berkeley's attack on this component consists of his arguments for his immaterialist thesis, *to be is to be perceived.* These were discussed above in Section 8.1.2. The conclusions there were that bodies are identical with collections of ideas ('Against the Strangely Prevailing Opinion'), and it that it impossible for objects to exist unperceived (the 'Master Argument').

If Berkeley's four-pronged attack on the representational theory of perception is on target, then that theory is in trouble. Berkeley's arguments should be taken seriously, for at the very least they force adherents of the theory to address certain perplexing questions. How do material objects cause ideas (mental states)? In what sense could something like an idea – a non-material entity – 'resemble' a material one? And what could it mean to say that material objects get perceived *through* sensory ideas? These perplexing questions continue to occupy philosophers and cognitive scientists today.

8.2.2. Defeating the sceptic, and returning to common sense

By now one might wonder how it is that Berkeley could advance himself as a champion of common sense. He denies the existence of an external world, and that denial seems wildly at odds with common sense. Berkeley must have been aware of this fact. Why, then, did Berkeley think that his philosophy is in accord with common sense?

This question, as we shall see, is a precursor to Berkeley's views about natural science, and his views about Newton's achievements in particular. There is indeed a perspective on the matter from which one might see Berkeley as a defender of common sense. He clearly believed that Locke's philosophy opened the door for scepticism. Locke endorsed the representational theory of perception, which allows the sceptic to question the existence of ordinary objects and our ability to know them. Locke also denied that we have *any* idea of matter and in effect claimed that matter is a theoretical entity (cf. Chapter 6, Section 6.1.3). Finally, Locke also conceded, as we have seen, that we have no understanding of how bodies cause ideas, or indeed any change at all (cf. Chapter 6, Section 6.1.4).

Berkeley thus saw the empiricist movement as leading directly to scepticism, and he believed that putting all reality within the perceptual grasp of human beings was the way to avert scepticism. Consider the following passages from the Third Dialogue:

> Since it is not a being distinct from sensations; a *cherry*, I say, is nothing but a congeries of sensible impressions, or ideas perceived by various senses . . . Hence, when I see, and feel, and taste, in sundry certain manners, I am sure the *cherry* exists, or is real; its reality being in my opinion nothing abstracted from those sensations.

> I am of a vulgar cast, simple enough to believe my senses, and leave things as I find them. To be plain, it is my opinion, that the real things are those very things I see and feel, and perceive by my senses [viz., ideas]. (WGB 2, 249)

From this perspective, there is nothing *about* which to be sceptical, for Berkeley lifted the epistemological veil between the perceiver and the real world. Common sense, it might be argued, dictates that the world is as we perceive it to be. And for Berkeley this is indeed the case: the real world *just is* what one perceives, namely, sensible ideas. Thus, if Berkeley is correct, there is no more wondering whether 'ordinary objects' exist, for if we perceive them, they exist: their *esse* is *percipi*.

It is perhaps this consideration that led Berkeley to conclude the *Dialogues* with the remark that 'the same principles which at first view lead to *scepticism,* pursued to a certain point, bring men back to common sense.' But there is more to be considered here, for Berkeley also lived, as we know, during a time of great scientific achievement. On the face of it, both mechanism and Newtonianism *appear* to posit the mind-independent existence of an external world, that is, objects with shape, mass and so on existing in absolute space. Even if there is a perspective from which Berkeley is a 'common sense' philosopher, the issue of how his immaterialism meshed with the new knowledge of the natural world calls for discussion. How did Berkeley's idealism square with the new science, and the knowledge it purports to yield?

8.2.3. Mechanism, Newtonianism and instrumentalism: Berkeley on the new science

Berkeley had a lot to say about how his idealism squared with the new science of his time. We are not in a position to discuss all of the details, but certain key elements should be noted in light of the developments of earlier empiricists.

Recall that most empiricists endorsed some version or other of *mechanism,* the view that all natural change can be explained in terms of the size, shape, motion and texture of matter. Clearly, Berkeley could not endorse mechanism *if* it were understood as positing the existence of mind-independent hunks of matter that cause our ideas. But he might nonetheless have endorsed an immaterialist version of mechanism. That is, he might have held that certain mechanical qualities of bodies – understood as collections of ideas – are regularly followed by others (ideas), and so the former explain the latter. After all, it is true even in Berkeley's world that billiard balls seem to cause other billiard balls to move. But all such claims in the hands of Berkeley, of course, must be understood in terms of ideas: certain *ideas* (billiard balls) are regularly followed by other ideas (other billiard balls). In other words, perhaps Berkeley could have agreed with his fellow empiricists that mechanism is a fruitful program for securing knowledge, but that it must be understood as applying to an immaterial world.

That something like this may have been Berkeley's view can be gathered from certain passages in the *Principles* and elsewhere. In Section 60 of the *Principles,* Berkeley anticipates the objection that on his view, there is no point to all the 'curious organization of plants, and the admirable mechanism in the parts of animals'. Recall that for Berkeley ideas are 'visibly inactive', for 'there is nothing of power or agency included in them', and therefore, 'one idea or object of thought cannot produce, or make any alteration in another' (*Principles* §25; cf. Section 8.1.1 above). For Berkeley, God is the immediate producer of all ideas. So, if the world consists of nothing but minds and ideas, and ideas are not causes of other ideas, what is the point of having, for example, a microscopic world of mechanical organization, for the latter is not productive of anything. The new science had discovered that there seems to be an underlying microscopic level that produces the macroscopic effects we see. But in Berkeley's world, the hands of a watch could continue to point to the numbers properly *even if* the watch had no springs, wheels, and so on inside of it, for the internal mechanics of the watch *do not cause* the hands to turn; God causes the hands to turn. So, the question for Berkeley is: what is the purpose of the world's microscopic mechanical organization if it does no work at all? How could Berkeley fit the microscopic level into his own views?

Berkeley addressed this objection directly and his answer reveals a unique perspective on the role of science:

But to come nearer the difficulty, it must be observed, that though the fabrication of all those parts and organs be not absolutely necessary to the producing any effect, yet it is necessary to the producing of things in a constant, regular way, according to the laws of nature. There are certain general laws that run through the whole chain of natural effects: these are learned by the observation and study of nature, and are by men applied as well to the framing artificial things for the use and ornament of life, as to the explaining the various phenomena; . . . And it is no less visible, that a particular size, figure, motion and disposition of parts are necessary, though not absolutely to the producing any effect, yet to the producing it according to the standing mechanical laws of nature. (*Principles* §62)

In this passage, Berkeley conceded that the microscopic mechanical organization of the world is not 'absolutely necessary' to the production of anything. Thus, 'absolutely' speaking, God could have made everything appear as it does with no underlying mechanical causes of what we perceive; God could have made the watch tick with no internal mechanism since the internal mechanism is not the cause of anything. Nonetheless, God produces ideas in a law-like fashion in order that humans can explain things, and use nature to their purposes. Presumably, if the watch did run without any internal mechanism, we would find this mysterious. Thus, God created a microscopic world of mechanistic parts in order for nature to be intelligible to finite minds, and that microscopic world of mechanistic parts is necessary in order for things to be produced in an intelligible and law-governed fashion.

But note that on Berkeley's view, even when explaining things according to the laws of nature, the mechanical philosopher is *not* in the business of identifying efficient causes of natural phenomena, contrary to what earlier empiricists maintained. Berkeley's view that ideas are 'visibly inactive' entails the view that there are no efficient causes in the phenomenal realm. Consider the following from the *Principles*:

[T]he connection of ideas does not imply the relation of *cause* and *effect,* but only of a mark or *sign* with the thing *signified.*

The fire which I see is not the cause of the pain I suffer upon my approaching it, but the mark that forewarns me of it. (*Principles* §65)

Nature, for Berkeley, presents us *only* with law-like successions of ideas, not causal connections between corporeal events. The fire does not *cause* pain in me, but constitutes only a 'sign' that pain will ensue. God is the cause of all of my ideas and 'signs', and has arranged things such that some ideas (pain) will follow others (fire). Accordingly, Berkeley tells us that the job of scientists 'with regard to their knowledge of the *phenomena*, . . . consists, not in an exacter knowledge of the efficient cause that produces them, . . . but only in a greater largeness of comprehension, whereby analogies, harmonies, and agreements are discovered in the works of nature' (*Principles* §105). Berkeley's scientist would not be someone who discovers efficient causes. He would only establish regularities for practical purposes (e.g. avoiding fires, nourishing the body etc.).

But does not this view of the scientist make Berkeley susceptible to the objection that according to his position, natural philosophy *explains* nothing, for it only reports regularities in the succession of ideas, and tries to subsume them under laws? If the fire does not *cause* the pain, the fire does not *explain* the pain, one might argue.

Here it is important to recognize a distinction in Berkeley between what we might call *mechanistic* explanation, and *causal* explanation. The mechanical philosophy, Berkeley allows, does provide a *sort* of explanation, and the following from *De Motu* makes this clear:

A thing can be said to be explained mechanically then indeed when it is reduced to those most simple and universal principles, and shown by accurate reasoning to be in agreement and connection with them. For once the laws of nature have been found out, then it is the philosopher's task to show that each phenomenon is in constant conformity with those laws, that is, necessarily follows from those principles. In that consist the explanation and solution of phenomena and the assigning their cause, i.e. the reason why they take place. (WGB 4, 41)

Here Berkeley allows for mechanistic explanation, which consists in showing that phenomena occur in accordance with, and can be predicted on the basis of, known laws of nature.

147

But Berkeley also emphasized in both the *Principles* and in *De Motu* that this mechanistic explanation is not true *causal* explanation. In *De Motu* §41, he writes that '[M]etaphysical principles and real efficient causes of the motion and existence of bodies or of corporeal attributes in no way belong to mechanics or experiment'. And in his work *Siris,* we find this:

> Certainly, if the explaining a phenomenon be to assign its proper efficient and final cause, it should seem the mechanical philosophers never explained anything; their province being only to discover the laws of nature, . . . and to account for particular phenomena by reducing them under, or shewing their conformity to, such general rules. (WGB 5, 111)

Mechanistic 'explanation', on this account, appears to be weak, for in order for an event to be truly *explained* (i.e. *causally* explained), one must cite its efficient and final cause, which mechanists do not, and cannot do, according to Berkeley.

So, Berkeley maintained that in order for a natural phenomenon to be causally explained, as opposed to merely mechanically explained, one must cite its efficient and *final* cause. Indeed, Berkeley was an advocate of final causes, as were Boyle and Newton before him:

> First, it is plain philosophers amuse themselves in vain, when they inquire for any natural efficient cause, distinct from a *mind* or *spirit.* Secondly, considering the whole creation is the workmanship of a *wise and good agent,* it should seem to become philosophers, to employ their thoughts . . . about the final causes of things: and I must confess, I see no reason, why pointing out the various ends, to which natural things are adapted, and for which they were originally with unspeakable wisdom contrived, should not be thought one good way of accounting for them, and altogether worthy a philosopher. (*Principles* §107)

Here Berkeley advocated the pursuit of final causes, or the goals or purposes associated with the law-like succession of ideas. This is not surprising: since God is the efficient cause of all our ideas and is a 'wise and good agent', he arranges the succession of ideas for certain purposes. For example, the heat of the fire has the purpose of warning me not to approach it too closely, and bread has the purpose of nourishment. A full account of any natural phenomenon will point out that it was immediately produced by God, and it will cite the purpose for which it was so produced.

That Berkeley thought this was the way to explain the succession of ideas is not surprising from another perspective, one having to do with his reaction to Newton's achievements. In the passages above, Berkeley's emphasis was on studying nature for its practical benefits, for learning the purposes of things, learning what ideas regularly follow certain others, and how humans may use this information for their own benefit. Indeed, it was Berkeley's general philosophy of science that science is primarily a *practical* endeavour and *not* one that gives us better approximations of physical reality. Recall that for Berkeley reality *just is* what the senses perceive, and there is no deeper account of nature (cf. Section 8.2.1 above). Thus, science should not have the goal of giving us better accounts of what physical reality is like, for common sense perception already tells us exactly what the 'physical' world is like.

All of this suggests that Berkeley was an *instrumentalist* about science. According to the instrumentalist, science only provides us with useful predictions for the purpose of managing our lives. On this view, scientific theories are merely convenient tools – *instruments* – that enable us to achieve certain ends. They are *not* the sort of things that describe physical reality in any deep sense, and any entities they refer to need not be understood as actually existing. This is most easily seen with respect to Berkeley's interpretation of Newtonianism.

As was noted in the last chapter, Newton appeared to claim that forces inhere *in* bodies. Berkeley, of course, could not take such talk literally, for he was committed to the thesis that bodies are collections of ideas, and ideas are entirely passive, or 'visibly inactive'. But this does not mean that Berkeley believed Newtonian theory was wrong. On the contrary, Berkeley was well aware of Newton's accomplishments, and praised him in a number of his writings. But Berkeley did have a specific interpretation of Newtonian theory, one that reflects his instrumentalism:

> *Force, gravity, attraction,* and terms of this sort are useful for reasonings and reckonings about motion and bodies in motion, but not for understanding the simple nature of motion itself or

for indicating so many distinct qualities. As for attraction, it was certainly introduced by Newton, not as a true, physical quality, but only as a mathematical hypothesis. (WGB 4, 35)

Berkeley here explicitly denied that the entities referred to in Newtonian theory exist. They are *not* real 'physical qualities', but only useful mathematical hypotheses. Berkeley was a Newtonian, but an unusual one. Since he denied the existence of a mind-independent world of bodies, he likewise denied the mind-independent existence of forces. Rather, Berkeley saw Newtonian theory is an *instrument*, a useful one, for managing our affairs. But even though Newton's theory was well confirmed and extremely accurate, Berkeley did not believe it committed him to the real existence of the entities to which it refers. It is for this reason that Berkeley could have believed that his interpretation of Newtonian theory resolved at least one crucial issue raised by Newton's work, and that is the issue of what kind of quality gravity is (cf. Chapter 7, Section 7.1.2). For Berkeley, gravity is not a real quality at all, but only a useful fiction that allows us to make nature intelligible and practical.

We have seen that Berkeley was open to mechanism, and thought highly of Newton's work. But we saw in the last chapter that Newton's work seemed to be at odds with mechanism, since mechanism could not explain the most fundamental force in Newton's world, the force of gravity. Although Berkeley was open to mechanism, it is worth noting that he seems to have been aware of the superiority of Newtonian theory over the earlier empiricist mechanism. He wrote in *Siris:*

Nature seems better known and explained by attractions and repulsions than by those other mechanical principles of size, figure, and the like; that is, by Sir Isaac Newton, than Descartes. (WGB 5, 116)

Here he referenced mechanism as it occurs in the writings of Descartes, but surely the point applies to all versions of mechanism.

8.2.4. Responses to popular objections

Because Berkeley's idealism is so counterintuitive, it is often the target of a number of objections. While I cannot address every objection to Berkeley's idealism, it is worth noting some of the more popular objections, primarily because Berkeley anticipated them, and his responses shed light on his thinking.

1. Unperceived Objects. The most popular objection to Berkeley is to his idealistic creed, *esse est percipi,* or *to be is to be perceived.* What about *unperceived* objects? That is, when I leave my office, and no one else is around to perceive my desk, does this mean that my desk ceases to exist?

Berkeley seems to have two responses at his disposal. First, in the *Principles,* he argued that a proper understanding of the word 'exists' yields the following: 'The table I write on, I say, exists, that is, I see and feel it; and if I were out of my study I should say it existed, meaning thereby that if I was in my study I might perceive it' (*Principles* §3). In other words, my desk exists even when no one is in the office because *if* I were to go into the office, *then* I would perceive it. While this might initially look like a promising response, it is not clear that it addresses the objection, for the desk still might not exist when no one is in the office. All that this response entails is that *it comes back into existence* when I enter my office.

A second response used by Berkeley in the *Dialogues* points out that there is *always* a perceiver, namely, God. We saw above (Section 8.1.1) that Berkeley offered arguments for the existence of God based on the idea that God is the best explanation for the cause of our ideas. In this context, God also plays the role of grounding the existence of objects that are unperceived by finite minds. This response may strike the contemporary reader as unsatisfactory, as it is only as good as the theistic arguments upon which it rests. Moreover, even if those theistic arguments are successful, a number of questions arise. For example, when we perceive the desk, we perceive sensory ideas. But according to traditional Christian belief, God, in virtue of being a perfect being, does not 'sense' in any straightforward way, let alone have sensory organs. How and whether this would get worked out is a consideration for the reader.

2. Do We All Perceive the Same Objects? A closely related objection stems from the fact that objects are collections of ideas for Berkeley. If this is true, one might argue that we *never* perceive the same objects. After all, I perceive a collection of ideas in *my* mind, and you perceive a collection of ideas in *your* mind, but they are never the *same* collection. When both of us are in my office, common sense dictates that we both perceive the *same* desk. But if Berkeley were correct, you perceive one collection of ideas (those in your mind), and I perceive another collection. Thus, we do *not* perceive the *same* objects.

Berkeley discussed this objection in the 'Third Dialogue', and his response was simple yet thought provoking. He distinguished between two senses of 'same', the 'vulgar' and the 'philosophical'. According to the former, it may indeed be said that we perceive the same desk. After all, we both point at it and converse about it rather easily. But in the philosophical sense of 'same', it may or may not be the case that we perceive the same desk. Berkeley argued that this is 'of small importance' since all that philosophers are doing in this context are quibbling about how to use the word 'same'. If we choose to use it in a strict philosophical sense, then indeed it may be said that we never perceive the same object. But Berkeley seems not to have been bothered by this consequence. Whether he should have been is an interesting question. It is worth noting in passing that an adherent to the representational theory of perception might have the same issue to contend with, for recall that according to that theory, even though there exist mind-independent objects, it is still the case that what we perceive directly are ideas, and no two people perceive exactly the same ideas.

3. Real vs. Imaginary Phenomena. One final popular objection has to do with distinguishing real phenomena from imaginary phenomena. If Berkeley were correct, and all objects are collections of ideas whose reality consists in being perceived, then does it not follow that the contents of dreams, hallucinations and other non-real things turn out to be *equally* real on Berkeley's terms? After all, these things are also ideas, according to Berkeley. One who admits the mind-independent existence of matter may be better placed to distinguish between real and imaginary phenomena, for she can simply distinguish between the two on the grounds that our ideas represent real things if those things exist independently of the mind, and our ideas do not, if there are no such mind-independent entities. But how can Berkeley make the distinction? If I perceive pink rats in my office, does it follow that they are as equally real as my desk, since both are mere collections of ideas?

This popular objection to Berkeley seems to have been anticipated by him in *Principles* §30:

> The ideas of sense are more strong, lively, and distinct than those of the imagination; they have likewise a steadiness, order, and coherence, and are not excited at random, as those which are the effects of human wills often are, but in a regular train or series, the admirable connection whereof sufficiently testifies the wisdom and benevolence of its author. (*Principles* §30)

Here Berkeley appeals to the fact that the objects of dreams and hallucinations are both less 'lively' than real things, and also they do not fit into fit into the 'regular train or series' of real ideas. In other words, they do not fit into our normal experience of the lawlike series of ideas that make up the natural realm. On this account, those phenomena that do not fit in with common sense, or the story told by science, are deemed imaginary. Of course, we might come up with extreme cases that challenge Berkeley's criteria here, but with respect to most cases, his way of distinguishing real from imaginary things seems plausible.

8.3. CONCLUSION: BERKELEY THE EMPIRICIST

Berkeley did not succeed in convincing many people of his idealism. Thus, it is not because of a large following that he is regarded one of the great classical empiricists. He is regarded as such for his sharp criticism of the empiricist movement up to that time, and for presenting a viable, if not popular, alternative for empiricists. In particular, he was a forceful critic of Locke, and in general succeeded in bringing to light the philosophical difficulties associated with the representational theory of perception.

But despite his differences with other empiricists, he was united with them in the belief that knowledge is based on sensory experience. From one perspective, Berkeley is more of an empiricist than those who came before, for what is presented to the senses *just is* the real world, and there is no other deeper reality to know. All empiricists prior to Berkeley also believed that knowledge is founded in experience, but also maintained a difference between reality as it appears to the senses and reality as it is in itself. The former represents the latter, but not always accurately. Berkeley's philosophy forces us to reconsider this dualism of appearances and the objective world in itself.

Thus, there is both a negative and a positive contribution by Berkeley. The negative consists of getting philosophers to reconsider their views about representational theories of perception. The positive consists of his presenting to us a viable alternative for an empiricist, a worldview consisting of nothing but minds and 'visibly inactive' ideas. Another positive contribution is the fact that he influenced David Hume, the subject of the next chapter.

CHAPTER 9

DAVID HUME (1711–1776)

David Hume was born in 1711 in Edinburgh, Scotland. His life largely overlapped with Berkeley's life. He was born within a year of the publication of Berkeley's *Principles,* and he was 16 years old when Newton died. Both Berkeley and Newton had a significant influence on his thinking. Hume is widely regarded the greatest empiricist that ever lived, and his work had a tremendous impact on twentieth century philosophy. His work on causation and induction are some of the most important contributions to the history of the philosophy.

Hume's father died when he was two years old, so he was raised under the Calvinist influence of his mother. It was apparent from his youth that he was exceptionally bright. He was educated at home until the age of 11 when he went with his brother to the University of Edinburgh. There he studied languages, philosophy and Newton's theories among other things. He left the University at age 15 without a degree, and shortly after leaving he began to have sceptical doubts about religion. This is significant not only because he was raised in a strict Calvinist environment, but also because he would be one of the first to systematically challenge the most popular argument for the existence of God at the time, the argument from design. This argument was endorsed in some form or other by Boyle, Locke, Berkeley, and especially Newton. Hume's book-length attack on the argument, *Dialogues Concerning Natural Religion,* was published after his death in 1779, and it is now a classic in the history of the philosophy of religion.

After leaving the University of Edinburgh, Hume entered an intense period of private study that precipitated his sinking into depression at the age of 23. He left the literary world for a job in commerce, serving as a clerk for a sugar merchant in Bristol. The depression passed quickly and in 1734 he travelled to France for a change of scenery. There he settled in the town of La Fléche, home of a famous Jesuit college. While he was there, he studied intensely and reportedly pestered the Jesuits with his sceptical arguments against religious belief. The most significant thing about his time in France is that during the years 1734–1737, Hume wrote one of his masterpieces, *A Treatise of Human Nature* (henceforth, the *Treatise*). He returned to England with the manuscript, and the work was published anonymously in 1739. The book was not well received, and the reviews were scathing. Hume famously complained about the work that it 'fell dead-born from the press'.

But the *Treatise* was not completely ignored. In 1745, the chair of Ethics and Philosophy became vacant at the University of Edinburgh, and Hume hoped to fill that position. By this time, he had already published, in 1741–1742, his work in moral and political philosophy, *Essays, Moral and Political*. But he was turned down by the Edinburgh town council due to his reputation, presumably based on his arguments in the *Treatise*, for being a sceptical atheist. Six years later he was again turned down for similar reasons from an academic post at the University of Glasgow. Despite his efforts, his reputation for being a religious sceptic prohibited him from ever attaining an academic post.

Shortly after being turned away from the chair at Edinburgh, Hume accepted a job as tutor to the Marquess of Annandale. He quickly regretted this decision as he discovered the Marquess was insane. A year later he took a job as secretary to his own cousin, Lieutenant-General James St. Clair. He accompanied St. Clair on missions to Ireland and Vienna, among other places. While Hume was in Italy in 1748, the work now known as *An Enquiry Concerning Human Understanding* (henceforth, the *Enquiry*) was published, the work upon which we shall focus in this chapter. It is a shorter, more accessible presentation of some of the more important ideas in the *Treatise*. Hume was apparently convinced that the lack of success of the *Treatise* was due to its manner of presentation, and so the *Enquiry* is a more popular reworking of the first part of the *Treatise*. In 1751, he published the *Enquiry Concerning the Principles of Morals,* which is also a reworking of certain ideas in the *Treatise*. Both works were better received, though not as well as Hume had hoped they would be.

His most popular work was not a philosophical one. Between 1754 and 1762, Hume wrote and published his six-volume *A History of England*. At the time, he was employed as a librarian to the Edinburgh Faculty of Advocates, and this provided him the resources to undertake such a big project. The *History* was a best seller, and earned Hume considerable financial stability. But shortly after the work was completed, Hume had to resign, for even as librarian he managed to offend the Library's trustees with his scepticism.

In 1763, Hume took yet another post, this time as private secretary to Lord Hertford, the Ambassador to France. Hume spent the next three years in France, enjoying a bit of literary fame and conversing with many French intellectuals. Indeed, he returned to England in 1766 accompanied by the famous French political philosopher, Jean-Jacques Rousseau. The friendship ended quickly, however, as Rousseau accused Hume of secretly trying to defame him. It seems Rousseau was suffering from paranoia, as there was no evidence to support the charges.

Hume spent the last few years of his life preparing new editions of his works, and composing and making plans to publish the *Dialogues Concerning Natural Religion*. In 1775, Hume became ill with a cancerous bowel, and began making preparations for his death. He died on 25 August 1776.

Throughout his life, Hume's philosophical views were widely criticized, and often kept him from earning and keeping employment. This was unfortunate, since history has shown that he was one of the most brilliant and influential philosophers to have ever lived. He made significant contributions to many areas of philosophy, but his chief contribution to the empiricist movement was a quasi-scepticism about the human ability to acquire knowledge of nature. The central core of his sceptical philosophy is his analysis of causation, and the closely related topic of induction. Hume is widely credited as the author of the now famous *problem of induction*. We will focus on that problem after beginning with the basics of Hume's worldview.

9.1. THE NATURAL REALM: HUME'S PSYCHOLOGICAL APPROACH

Hume is committed to the core empiricist thesis that all knowledge is founded in sensory experience. But the terminology he employs when presenting his empiricist views differs from that of earlier empiricists. Recall that earlier empiricists labelled the objects of perception 'ideas'. Hume deviated from this standard usage, and labelled all objects of the mind 'perceptions'. It is important to bear this in mind, as it has the potential to lead to confusion.

Like several earlier empiricists, Hume began his presentation by discussing the objects of knowledge, perceptions. He divides them into two kinds, *impressions* and *ideas*.

9.1.1. Impressions and ideas

Section II of the *Enquiry* is entitled 'Of the Origin of Ideas', and Hume's empiricism is there evident:

> Here therefore we may divide all the perceptions of the mind into two classes or species, which are distinguished by their different degrees of force and vivacity. The less forcible and lively are commonly denominated *Thoughts* or *Ideas*. . . . [On the other hand,] by the term *impression,* then, I mean all our more lively perceptions, when we hear, or see, or feel, or love, or hate, or desire, or will. And impressions are distinguished from ideas, which are the less lively perceptions, of which we are conscious, when we reflect on any of those sensations or movements above mentioned. (*Enquiry* §2)

There are two kinds of perceptions, ideas (or thoughts) and impressions. By the latter, Hume meant *present impressions*, and this is why they are considered the most 'lively'. In other words, he had in mind impressions *as they occur,* not as they are recalled. Note that according to Hume, one can have *inward* impressions as well as *outward* impressions. That is, one can have an impression of 'love' and 'desire' from inward *reflection,* and one can have impressions from outward *sensation,* such as vision.

Ideas, on the other hand, are 'less forcible and lively' than impressions, and they are any objects of the mind other than present impressions. For example, when we conjure up images of unicorns and past prime ministers, we are conjuring up ideas. Moreover, Hume famously maintained that all of our ideas are 'copies' of earlier impressions:

> In short, all the materials of thinking are derived either from our outward or inward sentiment: The mixture and composition of

these belongs alone to the mind and will. Or, to express myself in philosophical language, all our ideas or more feeble perceptions are copies of our impressions or more lively ones. (*Enquiry* §2)

Like earlier empiricists, Hume maintained that all 'the materials of thinking' come from experience, from 'our outward or inward impressions'. This entails that any ideas we employ must be 'copies' of our earlier impressions. For example, we can conceive of a unicorn, because we have had impressions of horses and animal horns, and we can join these ideas into one. Hume gave two arguments for this 'copy' thesis and its implication that all human knowledge and ideas are founded in experience.

First, Hume argued that an analysis of our ideas reveals that each one of them can be resolved into *simple* ideas that have their origin in – that is, have been 'copied' from – some former impression. For example, consider the complex idea of a white unicorn. It is a *complex* idea because it is composed of simple ones, such as the ideas of 'white', 'horse', 'horn' and so on Hume argued that all ideas are composed of simple ones of which we have had impressions. His argument is clear: consult your own perceptions and you will see that they can all be traced back to impressions. Even 'the idea of God, as meaning an infinitely intelligent, wise, and good Being, arises from reflecting on the operations of our own mind, and augmenting, without limit, those qualities of goodness and wisdom' (*Enquiry* §2). Thus, even complex ideas of which we have no direct impressions, such as God, can be broken down, according to Hume, to simple ones that are copied from prior impressions.

Second, Hume noted that people who suffer from a 'defect of the organ' do not have the ideas typically delivered by way of that organ. For example, those who are blind do not have ideas of colours, and those who are deaf do not have ideas of sounds. Hume argued that the best explanation for this fact is that all ideas come from inward and outward impressions. Such people are missing these ideas precisely because they are unable to receive the requisite impressions.

Hume was so confident of the accuracy of his empiricist picture that he suggested it could be used to test whether a term is being used meaningfully: 'When we entertain, therefore, any suspicion, that a philosophical term is employed without any meaning or idea (as is but too frequent), we need but enquire, *from what impression is that supposed idea derived?*' (*Enquiry* §2). And if we cannot assign an impression to a term, then we may rightly suspect that the term is without meaning. It is worth noting that this empiricist picture places Hume on Locke's side of the dispute over innate ideas (cf. Chapter 6, Section 6.1.1), though he does complain that Locke's attack on innatism lacked clarity and precision (cf. *Enquiry* §2, footnote).

9.1.2. The principles of association

Hume's empiricism was aimed at explaining how we acquire our ideas. But there is more to the story, since Hume believed 'that there is a principle of connexion between the different thoughts or ideas of the mind' (*Enquiry* §3). That is, a distinctive feature of Hume's empiricism, one that we do not find in earlier empiricists, is his attempt to explain how our ideas, once acquired, connect with each other. His account here is not theoretical, but is largely *psychological*. He believed that an examination of the contents of our own minds reveals that we naturally relate certain ideas together according to certain principles.

'To me', Hume wrote, 'there appear to be only three principles of connexion among ideas, namely, *Resemblance, Contiguity* in time or place, and *Cause* or *Effect*' (*Enquiry* §3). According to Hume, we connect our ideas together according to these principles:

> That these principles serve to connect ideas will not, I believe, be much doubted. A picture naturally leads our thoughts to the original [*Resemblance*]. The mention of one apartment in a building naturally introduces an enquiry or discourse concerning the others [*Contiguity*]: And if we think of a wound, we can scarcely forbear reflecting on the pain which follows it [*Cause* and *Effect*]. (*Enquiry* §3)

In this passage, Hume gave examples in order to demonstrate what he had in mind. If we see a picture of a place where we have vacationed, we naturally think of our vacation, and we do so because our ideas are governed by the principle of *resemblance*. We are the sort of psychological creatures who, when presented with an impression that resembles some other idea we have, naturally conjure up that other idea. If someone mentions an apartment in a building, this naturally leads us to consider what the others are like, and we do this because our ideas are governed by the principle of *contiguity*. The idea of salt often leads us to consider pepper, since these are so often found with each other contiguously in time and space. Finally, there is Hume's illustration of the principle of *cause and effect*. He noted that when we think of a wound, such as one caused by a knife, we immediately think of the pain that it must cause. Our thoughts are often connected on the basis of perceived causal connections.

It is important to note that Hume did not think he was giving a logical or philosophical account of the connections between our ideas. Rather, he was giving an empirical account of how, for better or for worse, our minds operate. These principles of association are important for Hume as they set the stage for his account of causation. The principle of cause and effect noted above played a crucial role in his account. But Hume never took his analysis beyond ideas and their connections, for he never presented a picture of the world as it is independently of our perceptions. Locke believed the world to consist of mind-independent hunks of matter, and Berkeley believed there was no mind-independent matter. Hume, on the other hand, took the empiricist line strictly: all we experience are perceptions, and speculations about what is beyond the content of our perceptions are unjustified.

9.2. KNOWLEDGE AND EXPERIENCE: HUME'S SEMI-SCEPTICISM

Hume made numerous contributions to the history of empiricism, but his analysis of our knowledge of causation is by far the most important. It has led many of his readers to conclude that Hume was a sceptic with respect to our knowledge of nature. At the very least, the analysis seems to entail that we are not capable of as much certainty about nature as previous empiricists believed we were. The analysis begins with Hume's distinction between two kinds of objects of human reason, *relations of ideas* and *matters of fact*.

9.2.1. Relations of ideas vs. matters of fact

According to Hume, 'all the objects of human reason or enquiry may naturally be divided into two kinds, to wit, *Relations of Ideas,* and *Matters of Fact*' (*Enquiry* §4). Relations of ideas are

'discoverable by the mere operation of thought, without dependence on what is any where existent in the universe' (*Enquiry* §4). In
other words, relations of ideas are known *a priori*, that is, independently of experience. For example, the truths of mathematics, such
as the proposition that 'three times five is equal to half of thirty',
are propositions which can be known without any empirical observation. They can be known simply by reflecting on the relationship
between the ideas contained in the proposition. One need not do
any empirical research to discover the truth of such a proposition,
and the opposite of every such proposition is a contradiction. The
same is true of the proposition, 'the sum of the interior angles of
every triangle is 180 degrees', which can be known simply through
the operations of thought, and to deny it is to contradict oneself.
Indeed, Hume noted that every mathematical truth expresses a
relation of ideas. These can be known with certainty.

Matters of fact, on the other hand, are such that their opposite
does not imply a contradiction, and so their opposite is still possible. In order to discover a matter of fact one needs to have the
relevant experience. In other words, they are known *a posteriori*, or
on the basis of experience. Consider the proposition, 'there are four
dogs in room 32.' One could not discover the truth of this proposition simply by reflecting on the relationship between 'dogs' and
'room 32'. Rather, one would have to experience room 32 in order
to see if it is true. Moreover, even if it were true, it is certainly *possible* that it is false, that is, one could easily imagine it being false,
unlike the truths of mathematics. Note that even truths to which
we are customarily used to believing can fall into this category. As
Hume, noted, '*That the sun will not rise tomorrow* is no less intelligible a proposition, and implies no more contradiction, than the
affirmation, *that it will rise*' (*Enquiry* §4). Although our experience
tells us that the sun comes up everyday, it is still conceivable that it
will not rise tomorrow, and no one could demonstrate (as one could
with mathematics) that it will rise. Hence, the belief *that the sun will
rise* is a matter of fact too.

Having made this distinction, Hume moves on to consider exclusively our knowledge of matters of fact, and its relation to cause
and effect. Relations of ideas, Hume believed, are demonstrable
and so are on firm footing. Matters of fact, however, cannot be
ascertained with the same kind of certainty, and this is important
for Hume, for matters of fact concern the very kind of knowledge

that earlier empiricists were concerned with, namely, knowledge of the natural world.

9.2.2. From matters of fact to cause and effect: Hume's first question

Note what Hume argued thus far. He distinguished between impressions and ideas, laid down the principles of association between ideas, and distinguished between the two objects of human reason, relations of ideas and matters of fact. Hume then asked a series of questions that brought all of this together for a sceptical conclusion.

Having laid the groundwork, Hume asked his first question:

> It may, therefore, be a subject worthy of curiosity, to enquire what is the nature of that evidence, which assures us of any real existence and matter of fact, beyond the present testimony of our senses, or the records of our memory? (*Enquiry* §4)

In other words, Hume asked the following question: What is the evidence that justifies us in believing the truth of any unobserved matter of fact, such as matters of fact concerning the future? It is important to emphasize that Hume was *not* raising a sceptical challenge here. Rather, he was simply inquiring about the nature of the evidence that leads us to believe propositions about things we have not observed. We all tend to believe the sun will rise tomorrow and that Newton's inverse square law will continue to govern nature next week. We feel that it is rational to believe such things, and Hume does not disagree. But the fact that we feel justified about such propositions concerning the future, about things no one has observed (indeed, they are unobserv*able*), calls for an explanation. Upon what evidence do we base such claims to knowledge? It is an innocent question, not a deeply philosophical one, and not a sceptical one.

Hume's answer is this:

> All reasonings concerning matter of fact seem to be founded on the relation of *Cause and Effect*. By means of that relation alone we can go beyond the evidence of our memory and senses. If you were to ask a man, why he believes any matter of fact, which is absent; for instance, that his friend is in the country, or

in France; he would give you a reason; and this reason would be some other fact; as a letter received from him, or the knowledge of his former resolutions and promises. A man finding a watch or any other machine in a desert island, would conclude, that there had once been men in that island. All our reasonings concerning fact are of the same nature. And here it is constantly supposed, that there is a connexion between the present fact and that which is inferred from it. Were there nothing to bind them together, the inference would be entirely precarious. (*Enquiry* §4)

Hume made the sweeping claim that *all of our reasoning about matters of fact is based on the relation of cause and effect.* Note Hume's examples: a person believes that her friend is in France *on the grounds that* she received a letter from the friend, grounds which involve the supposition that the letter she is holding was *caused* by her friend's mailing it from France. If the person did not believe there was a causal connection here, then the person would not have grounds for believing her friend is in France, that is, 'the inference would be entirely precarious'. A man who finds himself castaway on an island and finds a watch there would conclude others had been there. Why? Because he would suppose that some person had *caused* the watch to be there.

Hume gives other examples too. Suppose a person is in a dark room, and cannot see. Suppose further she hears a voice enunciate in English. She will conclude there is someone else in the room. Why? Because the sound of a rational voice is the *effect* of someone's talking. Two things are important to note about all of these cases: each involves believing the truth of an unobserved matter of fact (her friend is in France; others have been on the island; a person in the room), and each belief in these matters of fact presupposes knowledge or belief in certain causal relations.

9.2.3. Knowledge of cause and effect: Hume's second question

So Hume pointed out that knowledge of matters of fact presupposes a belief in the causal nexus of nature. The next line of inquiry, then, presented itself:

If we should satisfy ourselves, therefore, concerning the nature of that evidence, which assures us of matters of fact, we must enquire how we arrive at the knowledge of cause and effect. (*Enquiry* §4)

Having established that knowledge of matters of fact presupposes knowledge of causal relations, Hume began to inquire about our knowledge of causal relations: where does *this* knowledge come from, and what justifies us in our belief that there are causal relations in nature?

Recall that around the turn of the seventeenth century the idea of *force*, or *power* – that which is responsible for causal change – came under increasing scrutiny. Locke was sceptical about our having any idea of an active power in bodies (cf. Chapter 6, Section 6.1.4); Newton postulated the existence of forces in matter but remained silent on the nature of force as a quality of bodies (cf. Chapter 7, Section 7.1.2); Berkeley denied that Newtonian forces are real and gave an instrumentalist reading of Newton's work (cf. Chapter 8, Section 8.2.3). This discussion of force became a focus for Hume, who gave the most complete analysis of the notion of force, or power. Hume was aware of the controversy over the notion of force:

> There are no ideas, which occur in metaphysics, more obscure and uncertain, than those of *power, force, energy,* or *necessary connexion,* of which it is every moment necessary for us to treat in all our disquisitions. We shall, therefore, endeavour, in this section, to fix, if possible, the precise meaning of these terms, and thereby remove some part of that obscurity, which is so much complained of in this species of philosophy. (*Enquiry* §7)

Hume connected the notion of force with the issue of causation and this was a reasonable thing to do, for whatever kind of quality force is, it is what is supposed to be responsible for instigating causal change. Note that Hume employed the phrase 'necessary connexion' in the above passage. Hume was referring to a certain understanding of *causal* connections between events, or states of matter. It was widely believed that causal connections were *necessary* connections, those that relate two events in such a way that given the first (the cause), the second (the effect) *necessarily* occurs. Thus, in seeking to discover the nature of causation, Hume was analyzing the notion of force, or power, or necessary connection. So, a related

question is: what justifies us in believing that there are causal relations understood as 'forceful' necessary connections?

The first point that Hume made on his way to answering this
question was that knowledge of causal relations must be based on
experience:

I shall venture to affirm, as a general proposition, which admits
of no exception, that the knowledge of this relation is not, in any
instance, attained by reasonings *a priori;* but arises entirely from
experience, when we find, that any particular objects are constantly conjoined with each other. (*Enquiry* §4)

Knowledge of causal relations is not justified in the way that knowledge of relations of ideas is justified (cf. Section 9.2.1). That is, in
order to know that one thing c causes another e, it will not do *simply*
to reflect on c. Rather, one must experience c and its behaviour in
the natural world. If one has never encountered arsenic, one cannot know (leaving aside the testimony of others) that it will cause
death. To make his point clear, Hume used Adam – the Biblical first
man – as an example. 'Adam', Hume wrote, 'though his rational
faculties be supposed, at the very first, entirely perfect, could not
have inferred from the fluidity, and transparency of water, that it
would suffocate him' (*Enquiry* §4). Adam, Hume supposed, lacked
all experience, and so could not have known *in advance* – that is,
simply by reflecting on the concept of water, or even by empirical
examination of water by itself – that water would suffocate a person. Rather, this is something that Adam could only come to know
through experience. In general, Hume laid it down as an axiom *'that
causes and effects are discoverable, not by reason, but by experience'*
(*Enquiry* §4).

Another way that Hume made his point is through the following
example involving billiards:

When I see, for instance, a Billiard-ball moving in a straight line
towards another . . . may I not conceive, that a hundred different
events might follow from that cause? May not both these balls
remain at absolute rest? May not the first ball return in a straight
line, or leap off from the second in any line or direction? All these
suppositions are consistent and conceivable. Why then should
we give preference to one, which is no more . . . conceivable than

the rest? All our reasonings *a priori* will never be able to show us any foundation for this preference. (*Enquiry* §4)

Hume's point was that by *simply* reflecting on a billiard ball in motion (a cause), we can easily conceive that when it hits another billiard, both balls stop moving. Indeed, we can conceive indefinitely many effects: that the second ball explodes, or even turns into a chicken. The point is that without experience, we have no basis for 'preferring' one of these possible effects over another.

Hume's claim that we must look to experience to learn about causal connections seems obviously true, though it was not obvious to earlier mechanical philosophers, who seem to have believed that *purely* conceptual considerations about the size, shape, texture and motion of matter could reveal necessary causal connections between states of matter (e.g. Hobbes, Chapter 3, Section 3.2.2). After all, these are *mathematical* properties of matter, and the truths of mathematics are discovered through definitions and purely conceptual reasoning, or through relations of ideas. But Hume showed that experience is how we learn about causation.

So, what does experience tell us about causation? Does it reveal that there are necessary connections among events? Again, the inquiry here yields largely negative results, for experience does not, according to Hume, tell us much. We shall see in Section 9.2.5 more about what Hume believed it does tell us, but for now we focus primarily on what we do not learn about causation from experience.

For Hume and other empiricists, there are two sources of experience: sensation and reflection (cf. Section 9.1.1), that is, external and internal sense. Our belief that there are *necessary* causal connections is not justified *a priori*. So if it is justified, the justification must come from either sensation or reflection. With respect to external sense (sensation), Hume had this to say:

When we look about us towards external objects, and consider the operation of causes, we are never able, in a single instance, to discover any power or necessary connexion; any quality, which binds the effect to the cause, and renders the one an infallible consequence of the other. We only find, that the one does actually, in fact, follow the other. The impulse of one billiard-ball is attended with motion in the second. This is the whole that appears to the *outward* senses. . . . Consequently, there is not, in any single, particular instance of cause and effect, any thing which can suggest the idea of power or necessary connexion. (*Enquiry* §7)

Hume was more sceptical than any other empiricist about the senses' ability to give us any impression or idea of necessary connection. All that we sense when we see one billiard ball strike another is motion in the first and subsequent motion in the second. We do not receive any sensory impression of a necessary connection between them, of a force or power that binds the two events together. If we focus solely on the information provided by the senses, we get an impression of the first billiard ball striking the second, and then motion in the second. We receive no other impression that would give us any idea of necessary causal connections. In general, 'the scenes of the universe are continually shifting, and one objects follows another in an uninterrupted succession; but the power or force, which actuates the whole machine, is entirely concealed from us, and never discovers itself in any of the sensible qualities of body' (*Enquiry* §7, part 1).

But what about reflection? Do we receive any impression of power or necessary connection from our internal sense? It might be claimed that we do receive an impression of force or power from reflection on our own wills. That is, perhaps when one successfully wills certain movements of the body, this gives us an impression of power. When I decide to raise my arm (the cause), and my arm raises (the effect), do I receive an impression or idea of power (as Locke maintained – cf. Chapter 6, Section 6.1.4)? According to Hume, the answer is again negative:

The motion of our body follows upon the command of our will. Of this we are every moment conscious. But the means, by which this is effected; the energy, by which the will performs so extraordinary an operation; of this we are so far from being immediately conscious, that it must for ever escape our most diligent enquiry. (*Enquiry* §7, part 1)

Where Locke maintained that the activity of our will is the best source of our idea of active power, Hume denied that it provides any impression of active power. He denied this for three reasons (cf. *Enquiry* §7, part 1)

First, Hume argued that there is nothing more mysterious in nature than the influence of the mind over the body. This is particularly the case if one believes in the existence of the soul. The soul is typically understood as being the seat of our wills; it is the soul that causally influences the body. But how can a soul – an immaterial, non-extended substance – causally influence a material body? Hume argued that it is a mystery, and that therefore the power or connection by which this is done is also a mystery, and provides us with no clear impression of how it is done. In fact, Hume argued that it would not be any more mysterious if we were able to will the motion of a mountain. Whether it is a mountain or our own bodies, the connection between the two is equally mysterious. Many philosophers today would agree that the 'mind-body problem' (as it is called) is the biggest mystery confronting philosophers.

Second, Hume argued that it is equally mysterious that we can move some parts of our bodies but not others. 'Why has the will an influence over the tongue and fingers, not over the heart or liver?' (*Enquiry* §7, part 1) If we knew the answer to this, we would, presumably, know it on the basis of our knowledge of necessary connections. But the question and the mystery it points to only served to underscore our ignorance of the power of the will, or so Hume argued.

Finally, Hume drew on his knowledge of anatomy to argue that the immediate object of the will in cases of voluntary movement is not (say) the arm itself, but certain muscles and nerves which then transmit motion to the arm. So, although one wills the *arm* to raise, it is *not* the arm which is immediately effected. What is effected is 'another event, unknown to ourselves, and totally different from the one intended' (*Enquiry* §7, part 1). And so, Hume asked, how can we be conscious of a power to move our arms, when strictly speaking we have no such direct power, and any sense in which we do have it is wholly mysterious? 'We may, therefore, conclude from the whole, . . . that our idea of power is not copied from any sentiment or consciousness of power within ourselves' (*Enquiry* §7, part 1).

Hume went on to argue that similar considerations show that our ability to produce new ideas, as opposed to our ability to produce motion in our limbs, also provides us with no impression of power or necessary connection.

But even though we have no impression or idea of power or necessary connection, it is still on the basis of experience that we *attribute* causal connections between certain events. We believe that one billiard ball in motion is the cause of another because experience has always presented these two events together; the impact of a billiard ball in motion has always been followed by motion in the impacted billiard ball. And even though the two events are distinct, and not joined by any known necessary connection, we nonetheless label one the cause and the other the effect. And we do so on the basis of *experience*, or *past observation*. Thus, although we are not justified in believing in the existence of necessary connections, the beliefs we *do* possess of causal relations is based on past experience. In other words, what beliefs we do have of which events (e.g. heat) constantly follow others (e.g. fire) is based on past experience. *This* is the answer to Hume's second question: knowledge of causal relations is based on past experience, but causal relations are *not* 'forceful' necessary connections; they are distinct events that always accompany one another.

9.2.4. The problem of induction: Hume's third question

It would be convenient to summarize what has been established up to this point, and to recall that Hume's original question had to do with the justification of our knowledge of unobserved matters of fact, such as those about the future. Hume did just this in the beginning of Part II of *Enquiry* §4:

> But we have not, yet, attained any tolerable satisfaction with regard to the question first proposed. Each solution still gives rise to a new question as difficult as the foregoing, and leads us on to farther enquiries. When it is asked, *What is the nature of all our reasonings concerning matter of fact?* the proper answer seems to be, that they are founded on the relation of cause and effect. When again it is asked, *What is the foundation of all our reasonings and conclusions concerning that relation?* it may be replied in one word, EXPERIENCE. But if we still carry on our sifting humour, and ask, *What is the foundation of all conclusions from experience?* this implies a new question, which may be of more difficult solution and explication.

It has been established, according to Hume, that our belief in the truth of any unobserved matter of fact, such as matters of fact concerning the future, is based on the relation of cause and effect (cf. Section 9.2.2). And it has been established that any knowledge we have of cause and effect is based on past experience (but again, the relation between cause and effect does not involve power, or necessary connections; cf. Section 9.2.3).

But notice that in the passage above Hume asked the next logical question: '*What is the foundation of all conclusions from experience?*' In other words, what is the justification for drawing conclusions on the basis of past experience? It is crucial to understand how we arrived at this question, and why it is important. Hume explained:

It is allowed on all hands, that there is no known connexion between the sensible qualities and secret powers; and consequently, that the mind is not led to form such a conclusion concerning their constant and regular conjunction, by anything which it knows of their nature. As to past *Experience,* it can be allowed to give *direct* and *certain* information of those precise objects only, and that precise period of time, which fell under its cognizance: But why this experience should be extended to future times, and to other objects, . . . this is the main question on which I would insist. (*Enquiry* §4, part 2)

In this passage, Hume emphasized the importance of the issue. We began by asking about the justification for our belief that we have knowledge of unobservable matters of fact, such as those about the future. That led us to the answer that we believe them because of our past experience, but *not* the experience of necessary connections or 'secret powers' about causal relations; rather, the critical experience if of 'constant conjunctions'. I believe fire will be hot in the future (i.e. that these events, heat and fire, will be 'constantly conjoined'), and that billiard balls will continue to move other billiard balls because it has always happened that way according to my past experiences. Now Hume asked: *why am I justified in drawing conclusions about the future on the basis of the past?*

The question is *not* a sceptical one; it is a logical one. We all believe these things about the future, and Hume is *not* suggesting that we should suspend such beliefs. He is simply asking about the evidence for such beliefs: on what do we base such beliefs? Surely, we do not just pull them out of thin air, for we must believe them on the basis of some evidence. What is that evidence? The answer,

THE EMPIRICISTS: A GUIDE FOR THE PERPLEXED

it appears, is that we base them on past experience. But are we *justified* in drawing conclusions about the future on the basis of the past? Hume's answer: 'I say then, that, even after we have experience of the operations of cause and effect, our conclusions from that experience are *not* founded on reasoning, or any process of the understanding' (*Enquiry* §4, part 2). In other words, *there are no rational grounds* for drawing conclusions about the future on the basis of the past. Here is why.

When we draw conclusions about the future on the basis of the past, we do so, Hume argued, on the basis of the causal relations we have experienced in the past. We believe that fire will continue to cause heat in the future, and billiard balls in motion will continue to be causally effective in the future, because such causal connections have been found to obtain in the past. That is, we reason using *induction,* the very sort of reasoning recommended by Bacon (cf. Chapter 2, Section 2.2.2) and adopted by subsequent natural philosophers. Recall that in an inductive argument, one draws a conclusion about something unobserved on the basis of things observed in the past. So, according to Hume, when we reason that future causal regularities will be like past causal regularities, we reason thus:

(1) I have found that such an object (e.g. impact of billiard ball in motion; fire) has always been attended with such an effect (e.g. impacted billiard ball in motion; heat).
(2) Hence, similar objects (e.g. future impacts of billiard ball in motion; future fires) will be attended with similar effects (e.g. impacted billiard ball in motion; heat).

But clearly the argument is not logically valid. That is, the conclusion (2) does *not* follow from the premise (1); it does not *logically* follow that just because these things occurred in the past that they will occur in the future. Premise (1) does not provide support for conclusion (2).

To see this, note that the conclusion follows *only if* we add another premise (1.5):

(1) I have found that such an object (e.g. impact of billiard ball in motion; fire) has always been attended with such an effect (e.g. impacted billiard ball in motion; heat).

(1.5) The future will be like the past.
(2) Hence, similar objects (e.g. future impacts of billiard ball in motion; future fires) will be attended with similar effects.

If we add (1.5) to our argument, *then* the argument is sound, and we get the conclusion (2) that these things will occur in the future. Indeed, the person who reasons about the future on the basis of the past *must* be tacitly assuming the future will be like the past. Let us call the proposition that the future will be like the past (expressed in (1.5)) the *Principle of the Uniformity of Nature,* or PUN.

But the problem is that adding PUN to our reasoning is no solution at all, for the only argument available for PUN is of the *same form* as the argument above; it too is an inductive argument. In other words, the only argument available for PUN is the following inductive argument:

(1) I have experienced many pairs of events (causes and effect) that have been constantly conjoined in the past.
(2) Each time I found that similar pairs of events (causes and effect) were constantly conjoined in the future.
(3) Therefore, the future will be like the past. (i.e. PUN is true.)

This argument *also* is an inductive argument, for it *too* draws a conclusion about the future on the basis of past experience. But *any* argument that proceeds inductively suffers from the same problem: it tacitly assumes PUN. Indeed, it is unsound unless we add PUN as a premise. In this case, adding PUN as a premise yields the following:

(1) I have experienced many pairs of events (causes and effect) that have been constantly conjoined in the past.
(2) Each time I found that similar pairs of events (causes and effect) were constantly conjoined in the future.
(2.5) The future will be like the past.
(3) Therefore, the future will be like the past. (i.e. PUN is true.)

Clearly, this is a viciously *circular* argument, for the conclusion appears as one of the premises, and it violates logic for the conclusion to be identical to one of the premises. But only if we add the stipulation that the future will be like the past can we ever justify a belief about the future on the basis of past experience. Thus, we are caught in a circle, and Hume was the first to see it:

> We have said, that all arguments concerning existence [i.e. matters of fact] are founded on the relation of cause and effect; that our knowledge of that relation is derived entirely from experience; and that all our experimental conclusions proceed upon the supposition, that the future will be conformable to the past [i.e. PUN]. To endeavour, therefore, the proof of this last supposition . . . must be evidently going in a circle, and taking that for granted, which is the very point in question. (*Enquiry* §4, part 2)

This is the famous *problem of induction.*

Two points must be emphasized before moving on. First, one might think that as long as we believe the laws of nature are fixed for the future, we are justified in believing that future causal relations will be like past ones. But this will not work, because we can simply ask the question: what is the justification for believing that the laws of nature will obtain in the future? The only answer is to appeal to past experience. But if we do that, we are again caught up in the problem of induction since we are drawing a conclusion about the future on the basis of past experience. In short, the problem of induction applies to the laws of nature as well.

Finally, it is crucial to see the connection between Hume's analysis of causation and the problem of induction. Hume argued that there are no necessary connections between events. If there were necessary connections, then there might not be a problem with induction, for we would be justified in believing that future fires, for example, will cause heat on the grounds that there exists a *necessary* connection between fire and heat (in the way, for example, there is a *necessary* connection between '2+3' and '5', such that I know that 2+3=5 will be true tomorrow). If heat is *necessarily* connected to fire, then future fire will in fact generate heat. But there are no necessary connections. Thus, the problem of induction remains.

9.2.5. Hume's positive account of causation: induction regained?

Hume's analysis of induction has shown that induction is not rational, that our knowledge and expectations about the future are not based on the use of reason or logical argument. So, what *are* they based on? Why do we so firmly believe that fire will produce heat and the sun will rise tomorrow? What makes us form these firm convictions if it is not the use of reason?

Hume's answer was that 'all inferences from experience . . . are effects of custom, not of reasoning' (*Enquiry* §V, part 1). According to Hume, when we constantly witness 'constant conjunctions' of events, we become habituated to expect that those conjunctions will continue to occur in the future. In all our past experience, heat has always followed fire, and this forces us to develop the habit of attributing a connection between these two events, and to expect heat to follow fire in the future. Indeed, Hume argued that custom or habit is the 'great guide of human life':

> Custom, then, is the great guide of human life. It is that principle alone, which renders our experience useful to us, and makes us expect, for the future, a similar train of events with those which have appeared in the past. Without the influence of custom, we should be entirely ignorant of every matter of fact, beyond what is immediately present to the memory and senses. We should never know how to adjust means to ends, or to employ our natural powers in the production of any effect. There would be an end at once of all action. (*Enquiry* §5, part 1)

The principle of habit or custom, Hume believed, is not a bad thing. It is that which enables us to adopt our most important beliefs, and enables us to survive. In pointing out the principles of custom, Hume was giving us a positive spin on the sceptical line he advanced about induction. One way of seeing this is to take a look at Hume's positive account of causation.

As noted earlier, although the natural world does not present us with necessary connections, it does present us with causal relations, or constant conjunctions. That is, in Hume's words, certain events (fire and heat) are '*conjoined,* but never *connected*' (*Enquiry* §7, part 2). Still, *we* attribute connections between such events because after many repetitions we *feel* our minds make the transition from the thought of the first event to the thought of the second event. But the connection exists, as it were, only in our mind, for nature does not present us with connections: '[T]his connexion', Hume argued, 'which we *feel* in the mind, this customary transition of the imagination from one object to its usual attendant, is the sentiment or impression, from which we form the idea of power or necessary connexion' (*Enquiry* §7, part 2). When we are constantly presented with certain conjunctions of events, our mind transitions from one to another, and on the basis of this habitual transition that we feel, we form an idea of necessary connection, and attribute such connections to nature.

And for Hume, this is a justifiable practice, for nature does reveal some things about causal relations. For example, the objects believed to be connected are always contiguous in time and space; the cause is always prior to the effect; and of course, similar objects have been constantly associated in this way, that is, heat has always followed fire. These are things we do know, and on the basis of these observations, Hume gave his famous definitions of cause:

> Suitably to this experience, therefore, we may define a cause to be *an object, followed by another, and where all the objects, similar to the first, are followed by objects similar to the second.* Or in other words, *where, if the first object had not been, the second never had existed.* The appearance of a cause always conveys the mind, by a customary transition, to the idea of the effect. Of this also we have experience. We may, therefore, suitably to this experience, form another definition of cause; and call it, *an object followed by another, and whose appearance always conveys the thought to that other.* (*Enquiry* §7, part 2)

The first definition is based on what nature presents to us, while the second is based on our psychological selves: the appearance of a cause transitions our minds to thoughts about the effect.

This understanding of a cause and its relationship to the principle of custom or habit enables Hume to give something of a positive spin on the largely negative analysis of causation and induction. Although our belief in necessary connections is not logical or rational, Hume seems to have suggested that it is nonetheless *natural.* When we believe that future events will occur as they have in the past, such a belief is 'as unavoidable as to feel the passion of love . . . or hatred' (*Enquiry* §7, part 2). These beliefs 'are a species of natural instincts, which no reasoning or process of the thought and understanding is able, either to produce, or to prevent' (*Enquiry* §7, part 2). These beliefs are produced in us against our will – we do not choose to have them – and they are extremely useful. Thus, although Hume destroyed the logical-rational grounds of our belief in causal connections and future events, he may have restored a bit of justification for the practice of induction by pointing out its naturalistic grounds. Whether this is an adequate justification for our belief in induction is a perplexing issue left to the consideration of the reader.

9.3. CONCLUSION: HUME THE EMPIRICIST

Hume's empiricism is at once revolutionary and a natural result of what came before him. Newton struggled to give an explanation of gravity (cf. Chapter 7, Section 7.1.2), and Berkeley pointed out that our perceptions give us no idea of power or force; they are 'visibly inactive' (cf. Chapter 8, Sections 8.1.1 and 8.2.3). While Newton seems to have remained agnostic on the status of force, Berkeley was committed to God being the only causally active agent in the world.

Hume's work in some ways naturally follows this development. His commitment to empiricism led him to refrain from all discussion of whether there was an external world of bodies as Newton believed, and it also led him to agree with Berkeley that the contents of our perceptions reveal no impression of power, force, or necessary connection. But Hume was also a religious sceptic, and so was not prepared to posit God as the source of worldly power.

But even though Hume's work is in some ways a natural development of the empiricist movement, it is also revolutionary. His analysis of the notions of causation and necessary connection and their relation to the problem of induction was an unprecedented insight of perennial importance and a testimony to his genius. It had a tremendous impact on subsequent philosophy and discussions of causation and the rational grounds of induction continue to this day. Strict classical empiricism is usually seen an ending with Hume precisely because he took classical empiricism to its logical conclusion, a conclusion which forced subsequent thinkers to reconsider some of their most basic beliefs about the natural world.

CHAPTER 10

EMPIRICISM AND THE EMPIRICISTS: SUMMARY AND CONCLUSION

In the preceding chapters, I attempted to give an account of the empiricist movement from the seventeenth through the eighteenth centuries. I did not give the full account. The complete account is far too rich with details to be given in a single book. Still, I hope the account in the preceding chapters was enough to give a reasonably good feel for how classical empiricism emerged, and how it culminated in the work of Hume.

The movement began with the optimism of Bacon, who became increasingly convinced that rigorous experimentation, along with a proper method of induction, could produce knowledge of nature, and consequently a world in which we could manipulate nature for noble purposes. In doing this, he was revolting against the long standing Aristotelianism that had dominated up until his time. Hobbes agreed that knowledge must begin with close attention to sensory input from nature, but did not see the importance of experimentation. He did, however, offer a worldview based on mechanism, a world in which everything operates according to the pushes of matter in motion. In some respects, Gassendi and Boyle amalgamated Bacon and Hobbes: both advocated Baconian experimentation, and both advocated a mechanist worldview. But there were important differences, for Gassendi's mechanism involved a commitment to indivisible, intrinsically active atoms, while Boyle's mechanism was committed only to naturally occurring smallest parts of matter, corpuscles. These bits of matter were not necessarily indivisible, and they were not intrinsically active. The reasons that each of these early empiricists held these views are detailed in the early chapters of this book.

Just as Bacon had launched a revolution with respect to the method of knowledge acquisition, by the end of the seventeenth century, Locke and Newton had revolutionized closely related components of the empiricist movement. Although all philosophers who came before Locke were concerned with knowledge, Locke gave the first and most systematic analysis of knowledge. He produced a theory of knowledge with an eye to the mechanistic science that surrounded him, and one that would simultaneously justify and limit the new science of mechanism. Newton's accomplishments are well known, but the historical context in which he delivered his 'system of the world', and the philosophical questions it raised, are not as well known. He cast doubt on the mechanist movement, since forces, it appeared, are not explicable mechanically. And his work raised deep and perplexing philosophical questions about the status of gravity as a quality of objects. Indeed, it raised perplexing philosophical questions about the nature of the universe.

By the eighteenth century, thinkers such as Berkeley and Hume took empiricism to its logical conclusion. Berkeley focused on the empiricist claim, endorsed by nearly every seventeenth century empiricist, that we only have direct perceptual access to ideas, or sense impressions. He then argued that these ideas must *be* the objects of everyday experience of which we speak. It is not unreasonable to see Berkeley taking the empiricist line to where he believed it leads: if we are to focus on sensory experience, and sensory experience gives only ideas, then idealism is the only alternative. Thus, as we have seen, Berkeley developed a metaphysics, epistemology, and philosophy of science based exclusively on ideas and minds.

But when it comes to the claim that all knowledge is founded in experience, it is not difficult to see Hume as the biggest revolutionary. There is little evidence that empiricists before Hume saw the logical implications of empiricism that Hume pointed out. Empiricism culminated in Hume, and his work was largely destructive. He pointed out that almost everything previous empiricists thought we could know, could not be known on empiricist principles. Knowledge of religion, science, cause and effect, and (to some extent) the future all became problematic. But he not only argued for this scepticism; he argued for it *on the basis of empiricist commitments.* Hume showed where empiricism led, and it led, it seems, to a world where humans have very few rational grounds for the things they believe. There can be no doubt that Hume's work was revolutionary, and cast an entirely new light on the empiricist movement.

It would be wrong, however, to draw the conclusion that empiricism is no longer a viable alternative after Hume. Many versions of empiricism dominated early twentieth century philosophical thought, and many versions are accepted today. It is, after all, difficult to reject the thesis that sensory experience plays a significant role in the acquisition of knowledge and concepts. But no version of empiricism can ignore Hume's lessons. Indeed, I hope the book has shown that there are philosophical insights of perennial value in the hands of all the classical empiricists.

John Locke

Chappell, Vere. *The Cambridge Companion to Locke.* Cambridge: Cambridge UP, 1994.
Jolley, Nicholas. *Locke: His Philosophical Thought.* Oxford: Oxford UP, 1999.
Lowe, E. J. *Locke.* London: Routledge, 2005.

Isaac Newton

Cohen, I. Bernard and George Smith (eds). *The Cambridge Companion to Newton.* Cambridge: Cambridge UP, 2002.
McMullin, Ernan. *Newton on Matter and Activity.* Notre Dame: Notre Dame UP, 1978.
Cohen, I. Bernard and Richard Westfall (eds). *Newton.* New York: W.W. Norton, 1995.

INDEX

INDEX

BIBLIOGRAPHY

PRIMARY SOURCES

References in the text are keyed to the abbreviations below. Those works below followed by an asterisk (*) are available in many reprints both in printed versions and electronic form, as they are in the public domain.

WB: Bacon, Francis. *The Works of Francis Bacon.* Spedding, J., Ellis, R. and Heath, D. (eds). London: Longman and Co., 1858. Cited by volume and page number.

Principles: Berkeley, George. *A Treatise Concerning the Principles of Human Knowledge.* Dublin: J. Pepyat, 1710. Cited by section number. (*)

WGB: *The Works of George Berkeley,* A. A. Luce and T. E. Jessop (eds). (London: Nelson, 1948–1957). Passages are cited by volume and page number.

Stewart: Boyle, Robert. *Selected Philosophical Papers of Robert Boyle.* Stewart, M. A. (ed.). Indianapolis: Hackett Publishing, 1991. Cited by page number.

SWG: Gassendi, Pierre. *The Selected Works of Pierre Gassendi.* Brush, C. (ed.). New York: Johnson Reprint Corporation, 1972. Cited by page number.

EW: Hobbes, Thomas. *The English Works of Thomas Hobbes.* London: John Bohn, 1966. Cited by volume and page number.

Enquiry: Hume, David. *An Enquiry Concerning Human Understanding.* London, 1748. Cited by section number. (*)

Essay: Locke, John. *An Essay Concerning Human Understanding.* London, 1690. Cited by book, chapter, and section number. (*)

Janiak: Newton, Isaac. *Philosophical Writings.* Janiak, A. (ed.). Cambridge: Cambridge UP, 2004. Cited by page number.

SECONDARY SOURCES AND SUGGESTIONS FOR FURTHER READING

Francis Bacon

Gaukroger, Stephen. *Francis Bacon and the Transformation of Early Modern Philosophy.* Cambridge: Cambridge UP, 2001.

Peltonen, Markku (ed.). *The Cambridge Companion to Bacon*. Cambridge: Cambridge UP, 1996.

George Berkeley

Fogelin, Robert J. *Berkeley and the Principles of Human Knowledge*. London: Routledge, 2001.
Muehlmann, Robert G. *Berkeley's Ontology*. Indianapolis: Hackett, 1992.
Turbayne, Colin (ed.). *Berkeley: Critical and Interpretive Essays*. Minneapolis: Minnesota UP, 1982.
Winkler, Kenneth P. (ed.) *The Cambridge Companion to Berkeley*. Cambridge: Cambridge UP, 2005.

Robert Boyle

Anstey, Peter. *The Philosophy of Robert Boyle*. London: Routledge, 2000.
Hunter, Michael (ed.). *Robert Boyle Reconsidered*. Cambridge: Cambridge UP, 1994.
Sargent, Rose-Mary. *The Diffident Naturalist: Robert Boyle and the Philosophy of Experiment*. Chicago: Chicago UP, 1995.
Wocik, Jan. *Robert Boyle and the Limits of Reason*. Cambridge: Cambridge UP, 1997.

Pierre Gassendi

Joy, Lynn S. *Gassendi the Atomist*. Cambridge: Cambridge UP, 1987.
Lolordo, Antonia. *Pierre Gassendi and the Birth of Early Modern Philosophy*. Cambridge: Cambridge UP, 2007.
Osler, Margaret. *Divine Will and the Mechanical Philosophy*. Cambridge: Cambridge UP, 1994.

Thomas Hobbes

Martinich, A. P. *Hobbes*. London: Routledge, 2005.
Missner, Marshall. *On Hobbes*. Belmont: Wadsworth, 2000.
Sorrell, Tom. *The Cambridge Companion to Hobbes*. Cambridge: Cambridge UP, 1996.

David Hume

Noonan, Harold. *Hume on Knowledge*. London: Routledge, 1999.
Norton, David F. *The Cambridge Companion to Hume*. Cambridge: Cambridge UP, 1993.
Radcliffe, Elizabeth. *A Companion to Hume*. New York: Blackwell, 2008.